TOUCH OF
DIVINE
WISDOM

Paramhansa Yogananda

T**O**UCH OF DIVINE WISDOM

LIVING THE TEACHINGS OF

Paramhansa Yogananda

NAYASWAMI JYOTISH
AND NAYASWAMI DEVI

CRYSTAL CLARITY PUBLISHERS   Commerce, California

CRYSTAL CLARITY PUBLISHERS
1123 Goodrich Blvd. | Commerce, California
crystalclarity.com | 800.424.1055
clarity@crystalclarity.com

ISBN 978-1-56589-099-2 (print) | CIP available
ISBN 978-1-56589-591-1 (e-book) | CIP available

Cover layout design and interior design by Tejindra Scott Tully
Interior layout by Michele Madhavi Molloy
Cover image by lifeforstock on Freepik

The Joy Symbol is registered by
Ananda Church of Self-Realization
of Nevada County, California.

CONTENTS

ART AND PHOTO CREDITS

The paintings you're about to enjoy in a number of these blogs were all done by Nayaswami Jyotish. We list each of them here along with its page number and a link you can use to view it as a larger image and, if you'd like, to purchase it as a print. These are just a few of Jyotish's many paintings; you can see them all at crystalclarity.com/111.

PHOTO CREDITS

We offer grateful appreciation to the many Ananda residents who over the years have contributed photographs to the Ananda Image Library. Almost all the photos in the book that aren't listed below were taken from that library. A handful of others are in the public domain.

PREFACE

*T*ouch of Divine Wisdom is a compilation of our weekly blogs written during the year 2021. It's amazing to us that we're already up to the fifth book in this series, preceded by *Touch of Light*, *Touch of Joy*, *Touch of Love*, and *Touch of Peace*. We've been sharing weekly for almost ten years now, with a total of nearly five hundred blogs. When we began writing rather lightheartedly in 2013, we had no idea that such a large, appreciative, and worldwide group of readers would be enjoying them.

In *Touch of Divine Wisdom*, we focused on themes we hoped would offer our readers understanding, inspiration, strength, and hope to deal with the challenges they might be facing. Wisdom is different from mere knowledge, for it penetrates beneath the surface of things to perceive their underlying reality. Wisdom offers practical solutions, where the rational mind may see nothing but problems. It declares: "There are no such things as obstacles: There are only opportunities!"

Swami Kriyananda, our lifelong teacher, occasionally had us present in the room when he counseled people. He often told us, "Listen to what they are asking behind the words they use. Once you understand what they are really asking, then feel intuitively what to say to them." He defined wisdom as a combination of mind and heart, of discrimination and love.

As we travel around the world, we see that there are common questions for which many people are seeking answers. We respond to them in our blogs using the vast store of spiritual and practical teachings of our guru, Paramhansa Yogananda. We draw also from our personal experiences of more than forty years with Swami Kriyananda, a direct disciple of Yogananda, and as leaders and teachers for Ananda, the worldwide organization that he founded. Ananda has now spread around the world to many cultures in dozens of countries. It is a living laboratory demonstrating, as Yogananda once forcefully declared, that "Simple living plus high thinking lead to the greatest happiness."

In closing, we want to thank our copy editor, Nayaswami Lakshman, and our layout artists, Kalamali and Nara Bedwell, for their invaluable help. The "*Touch*" series would not be possible without them.

Each blog is a blend of deep philosophy, practical tips, and humor: a combination, in fact, of our hearts, minds, and souls. We sincerely hope that you will enjoy the "*Touches*" *of Divine Wisdom* you will find in these pages.

NAYASWAMI JYOTISH
NAYASWAMI DEVI
Ananda World Brotherhood Village
February 11, 2023

TOUCH

of

DIVINE
WISDOM

IN LOVE AND APPRECIATION

Paramhansa Yogananda's birthday is January 5. Usually we give people presents on their birthday, but what do you give to someone who has everything? who is everything? No choice is left us but to offer our love and appreciation. This is all we can truly give, and the hidden gift behind all outward symbols.

In a spirit of appreciation, then, I'd like to share how Yogananda's qualities have helped shape my life. Master said that he particularly manifested three of the eight aspects of God: wisdom, love, and joy. As I try to attune my will with his, I let these three qualities be my primary guides. Here are some ways that I do this.

"Grand Canyon," by Nayaswami Jyotish.

First, let's consider wisdom: Swami Kriyananda said that wisdom is different from intellect or discrimination. Wisdom springs from a combination of heart and mind. You need both qualities truly to understand anything or anyone. As the great botanist George Washington Carver once said, "Anything in nature will speak to you if you love it enough."

There are many ways to tune in to Yogananda's wisdom, especially through reading his numerous books, lessons, and talks, but lately I've hit upon a new one. I've read that he considered three books to be scripture: the Christian Bible, the Bhagavad Gita, and his own book of prayer demands, *Whispers from Eternity*. *Whispers* is a treasure chest of wisdom. It combines deep devotion — the highest form of love — with sensitive guidance showing the appropriate attitudes to hold in most any circumstance. I have started reading and meditating on a different one of these prayers toward the end of each meditation. It is proving to be an absolutely marvelous practice.

Next, there is love: This is one of the most powerful forces in creation. It is the vibration that brings about union, and it expresses itself in various forms in all human relationships. But it is a much more universal force than just this. It is the power that holds atoms together and keeps planets in their orbits.

I've found that one of the best ways to feel and express love is through kindness expressed as friendship. Swami Kriyananda was a model in this. I've seen instances where virtual strangers immediately felt his love and friendship and wept when he was about to leave. Why? Because he was constantly radiating love and friendship like a surrounding aura as he went about his daily business. People felt it and it changed their lives.

Finally, let's talk about joy: Joy is constantly flowing within us as part of our very being. We don't have to try to feel joy, we just need to become aware of its constant presence. It is like feeling your heartbeat: You can sense it as soon as you become calm and pay attention. Feel joy toward the end of each meditation and try to expand it. Then keep an awareness of that feeling throughout the day.

It is said that imitation is the sincerest form of flattery. The best way to imitate Yogananda is to feel ourselves swimming in a sea of wisdom, love, and joy. Do this and don't worry about anything else. The mere act of attunement will take care of all the details.

In love and appreciation,
NAYASWAMI JYOTISH

DEALING WITH CHANGE AND LOSS

There's a joke about a man who woke up one morning to discover that he had only three, long hairs left on his head. As he looked into the mirror, he said, "Today I think I'll wear my hair in a braid." The next morning he found that he had only two hairs left and thought, "Hmm . . . today I'll part it down the middle." On the third day there was only one hair left, so after some thought, he decided to wear it in a ponytail.

Finally on the fourth day there were no hairs left at all. He sighed with relief. "Thank goodness. Now I don't have to worry about how to wear my hair anymore!"

I hope this story brought a smile to your face, but there's a deeper message in it as well. Change and loss are an inevitable part of life. We can't escape them, but we *can* choose how we deal with them. We can go the route of resentment, blame, and self-pity when faced with difficulties; or we can accept them willingly with openness and a positive expectation. It all depends on our level of consciousness.

In *Whispers from Eternity*, Paramhansa Yogananda writes: "We must prepare ourselves mentally to meet life's inevitable trials, difficulties, and tragedies. For such preparation, the movies we see in actual theaters can be instructive. If viewed with inner calmness and detachment, they can help us to understand that nothing in life is real in itself." "*The fundamental cure for all human ills is everywhere one and the same: to raise one's consciousness.*"

Let's look at some changes that most of us face — loss of material possessions, health challenges, the passing of loved ones — and find ways to rise above the suffering they bring.

From personal experience, I've learned that even in the midst of losing everything one owns, it's still possible to find a center of peace and security within. Our drama unfolded in July 1976 when a forest fire swept through Ananda Village, destroying hundreds of wooded acres and most of the community's buildings, including our home and everything we owned. This happened at a particularly vulnerable time for us: Our son had been born just eleven days earlier.

With nothing but the clothes on our backs, we prayed to God for the strength to face the future. In response, we felt uplifted by an understanding that the source of our security and well-being was not our possessions, but an inner connection with God. Over time we came to realize that losing everything we owned was one of the greatest inner gifts we'd ever received, because on some level it permanently freed us from dependence on material things for our sense of well-being.

Another challenge that everyone deals with, especially now during the pandemic, is the loss of good health. Swami Kriyananda, who faced an almost constant series of health challenges, was a wonderful model for how to deal positively with them. We were with him before and after many surgeries, and his unwavering attitude of calm inner joy was astonishing.

How did he do this? We could see that there was never any denial of the situation, but rather complete acceptance and almost embracing of what was happening. He also maintained an inner detachment from his body, as though he were thinking, "This illness may be happening to my body, but it doesn't touch my true reality, my soul nature." Through all the tests and trials he confronted in his life he had unwavering trust and faith in his guru to sustain him.

Probably the hardest loss to deal with is the death of friends or loved ones. Yoganandaji faced overwhelming grief with the passing of his mother when he was a young boy. Inconsolable for many years, he was finally comforted by the voice of Divine Mother, who said: "It is I who have watched over thee, life after life, in the tenderness of many mothers! See in My gaze the two black eyes, the lost beautiful eyes, thou seekest!"

We can find comfort from such a loss by looking past the form of our loved one to the One Beloved hidden there.

Let's embrace all the changes and losses in life with the uplifted consciousness and strength of divine warriors.

"It is God alone who acts through you," Yoganandaji said. "It is Him alone you should really love—through others, when you love them. People aren't aware of that great, ever-comforting presence. They focus all their affection on one another. When someone whom they love dies, they think, 'Oh, how cruel!' But it was God alone all the time, playing at hide-and-seek with them!"

Let's embrace all the changes and losses in life with the uplifted consciousness and strength of divine warriors. Then we can stand firmly in the truth that no loss can dim the light of God that shines within us and within everything in this world.

May you find God's peace in the midst of change.

NAYASWAMI DEVI

HOPE FOR A BETTER WORLD

We have occasionally written about the devastating forest fire of 1976, which destroyed our home along with most of the other houses at Ananda Village. We awoke that morning to a normal day with its usual routine, but within a few chaotic hours we had lost our home, our possessions, and our security. How can we look back through the telescope of time and view this as one of the best days of our life? Well, let me explain.

People usually try to find their solutions by changing their circumstances: Perhaps a big insurance settlement would have given us back our security. Or, in today's world, maybe a vaccine will cure our sickness; or economic stimulus, or a new political regime will fix our problems. But Swami Kriyananda's response to Ananda's crisis gives us a different approach, one that truly offers hope for a better world.

He knew that for lasting solutions, we needed to reach beyond ourselves: to expand our hearts and to serve others. Almost as soon as the ashes had settled and the smoke had cleared, Swamiji began to talk about going on a nationwide tour. The more practical-minded residents wondered, How could a lecture tour possibly help us rebuild our houses or replant our forests? Moreover, they reasoned, it was certain to lose money, which we desperately needed for new homes. Well, those critics were right on a "practical" level, but so wrong on deeper levels.

Swami bought a motor home, and with a small group of singer/helpers began to crisscross the country with the "Joy Tours." He lectured in most of America's major cities just as his guru, Paramhansa Yogananda, had done nearly a half-century earlier. The major theme during that tour was that learning to live in joy is the *solution* to problems, and that only by uplifting our consciousness can we realize our dreams.

A better future comes when we expand and elevate our consciousness.

Now, a half-century later, we find ourselves needing solutions to another crisis: the chaos of the pandemic and the resulting economic and political disruption. This time we need to rebuild not just one community, but the whole world. The answer, my friends, is the one Swamiji showed us — the one that has worked since the beginning of time. A better future comes when we expand and elevate our consciousness. Our hopes for a better world will be realized only as we ourselves become more realized.

Each day I have been reading and meditating on a different prayer-demand from Paramhansa Yogananda's *Whispers from Eternity*. Today, I read the perfect answer to the problems that plague the world, his "Prayer for expanding Love from myself to all my brethren." It begins with these immortal words:

O Divine Mother, teach me to use the gift of Thy love, which I feel in my heart, to love the members of my family more than myself. Bless me, that I may love my neighbors more than my family. Expand my heart's feelings, that I may love my country more than my neighbors, and my world and all my human brethren more than my country, neighbors, family, and my own self.

Lastly, teach me to love Thee more than anything else, for it is only Thy love that enables me to love everything. Without Thee, I could not love anything or anybody.

Yes, we should do everything we can to improve this world on a practical level. But lasting solutions come only from expanding the aura of our love and by living in joy.

In joy,
NAYASWAMI JYOTISH

KEEPING YOUR BALANCE

recently read an article by a dance teacher that gives us surprisingly helpful advice about how to deal with life's challenges. The instructor, Jan Erkert, wrote: "As a dancer, I study physical states of energy. In one exercise I often conduct with my students, one dancer must remain still while others throw their full weight into them, like football without any protection. Most fall into a heap on the floor with one or two hits. But one woman I once taught could do it. She was 4'9" and weighed less than ninety pounds, yet as the dancers hurled themselves into her, they bounced right off. She knew something they didn't. Calm is deceptive. From the outside, it looks still. But within the body, it is anything but. Every time she was hit, she recalibrated and adjusted her weight. It was subtle and easy to miss the astounding skill [involved]. Calm isn't the lack of energy, but rather fluid energy arrested."

I found her description fascinating and, as I said, extremely help-ful in dealing with karmic body blows. The chain of cause and effect that we ourselves set in motion usually takes some time to return to us. Thus, we will be faced with situations that have the *potential* to affect us, but haven't yet become fully manifest. And then there are those tests that are *already upon us*, and demand our immediate response.

To deal with potential blows, let's remember the example of the dancer and practice the art of inner micro-adjusting. Look at common traps that you fall into, and be prepared to recalibrate your reactions: to adjust your attitudes, thoughts, or words before you get caught.

Do you often react to certain challenges with anger, or judgment? with blaming others, or self-justification? When you feel a recurring karmic situation moving towards you, make the necessary mental or behavioral adjustments while you are still free to do so. The more you can self-adjust early in the process, the less power karma will have over you. Catch yourself before you blow up, or condemn others. Control your energy and return to a state of balance. Over time you will find yourself freer from that particular karma.

When you find yourself already in the midst of a big test, you can still apply the same principle. In the Bible, Jesus Christ states: "I say unto you, that you resist not evil; but whosoever shall smite thee on thy right cheek, turn to him the other also." His words are generally taken as advice to be passive and contrite in the face of aggression. But Yoganandaji gives a very different interpretation: Christ is talking about the law of karma. If a blow is coming to you, don't tense up and resist it, but think, "Bring it on!" Welcome it and respond like the centered dancer who saw her assailants bounce off of her. It all comes down to staying centered in the calm eye of any karmic storm.

In *Whispers from Eternity*, Yoganandaji wrote: "Throughout all trials, of whatever nature, we can retain our equilibrium and sail through the most harrowing experiences with our inner peace and joy unaffected, if we remain inwardly calm. Learn to look upon whatever happens to you with the certainty that nothing can touch you in your true, inner Self: your soul."

To paraphrase the dance teacher, Calm isn't the lack of energy: It is learning to control your reactions and the flow of inner energy. When bad karma comes, as it inevitably will until we are free souls, don't let it slam you to the ground.

Through a regular practice of meditation, we become more absorbed in the calmness of our soul nature. Learn to live in that calmness, and keep your balance in all circumstances. Then you will find yourself dancing gracefully through life hand in hand with your unseen partner, God.

With joy,
NAYASWAMI DEVI

PEACE

evi wrote her last blog on the subject of calmness, saying, "When you feel a recurring karmic situation moving towards you, make the necessary mental or behavioral adjustments while you are still free to do so. The more you can self-adjust early in the process, the less power karma will have over you." This is the proper way to fight our karmic battles. But there are times when the wiser decision is to sign a peace treaty, and withdraw from all activity.

At first glance, peace and calmness — two of the eight qualities of God — might seem similar, but they are actually quite different. Swami Kriyananda states it this way: "Peace is the soothing cessation of all agitation of feeling, whereas Calmness is dynamic, and is the silent, essential core of creativity, of impersonal love, and of divine wisdom."

Each of these "attitudinal tools" is needed at different times, just as a carpenter's tool belt needs both a hammer and a saw. Calmness is good during activity, but peace, like sleep at night, won't come until we relax.

There is a wonderful true story that illustrates the peace that comes at the cessation of conflict. It is December 1914, five months into the First World War, and more than a million young men have died. The two sides have burrowed into opposing trenches, with a deadly no-man's land in between. On Christmas Eve, the English hear hundreds of German voices singing "Stille Nacht, Heilige

Nacht." The English respond by singing "The First Noel," and "Silent Night." Enthusiastically, joyfully, each side applauds the efforts of the other. Late into the night they trade carols, finally singing in unison. Then, opposing soldiers from each side come out of their trenches to exchange gifts, preciously hoarded food items, and photos of loved ones. They even worship together and say last rites for the dead of both sides. Alas, the next morning, obeying their leaders, they resume the bloody battle.

For a few short hours the unifying Christ consciousness had worked the miracle of peace. We, too, would do well to learn the art of declaring peace when we find our minds filled with projects and worries, strife and negativity. Does all that mental activity really bring us happiness?

How can we achieve inner peace? It is easiest to find in the stillness of deep meditation. If you calmly observe your thoughts and emotions, they will begin to diminish like mist under the morning sun. When you observe some whirlpool of thought or feeling, simply let it fade away. Those of you who practice the *Hong-Sau* technique of watching the breath will already have developed these skills.

As you continue to withdraw, you will see into more and more subtle areas of your mind. Let it all go! In inner stillness you understand that while your ego wants to stay restless, your soul wants to rest in the peace of God. Gradually, peace becomes supremely attractive, and you will no longer want to return to the "no-man's land" of worldly pulls.

Our inner attitudes will magnetize outer changes also. If you have an aura of peace, the whole world will become peaceful in your presence. The former "enemies" that disturbed you will no longer feel the need to defend themselves. Then friendships will return, mutual laughter will replace old hurts, and the gentle beauty of peace will spread like wildflowers in spring.

In peace,
NAYASWAMI JYOTISH

THE LIGHT SHINING IN DARKNESS

have a confession to make. There are times when I can become stubborn. I expect this can be a little challenging for my friends, but at times it has produced some interesting results.

Here's an example. While in college my friends and I would occasionally sign up as subjects for psychology experiments. These were harmless enough, and we got paid for our time. We actually came to enjoy them, because the psychologists never told us what they were really studying, so we had to guess the true focus of their research.

During one such experiment, the psychologist brought me into a room which was empty except for a chair placed in the middle. After I got settled on it, she shut the door, turned off the lights, and left me sitting alone in complete darkness. Then a disembodied voice from another room said, "The object of our experiment is to see if the eyes can track movement of a point of light in complete darkness."

A point of light suddenly appeared before me. I focused on it, trying to sense any movement. To help orient my perception, I extended my arm with my thumb pointed upward and placed it next to the tiny point. Although I couldn't see my thumb, I could sense its relation to the light. In this way I could track any movement by the distance of the light from my thumb.

Then the voice said, "Now, tell us if the light is moving to the right or left." By keeping my arm steady, I could tell the light had remained stationary. "It's not moving either way," I said. The voice replied, "It *is* moving. Tell us in which direction."

"Sorry," I said, "it's *not* moving." This exchange went on several more times. Finally, with a deep sigh, the researcher said, "Okay, now tell us in which diagonal direction the light is moving."

Still keeping my arm and thumb fixed in a position next to the light, I could tell there wasn't any movement, and I wasn't about to be deterred. There I was, alone in a totally dark room, but still, after each of several attempts to convince me otherwise, I replied, "Sorry, but it's *not* moving."

At this point the disembodied voice became totally silent. I waited for a while and finally said, "I don't care if you never let me out of this room: The light has *not* moved." After another period of silence, the lights in the room came on, a door opened, and a very frustrated-looking psychologist entered.

Somewhat embarrassed, she confessed, "You were right. The light wasn't moving, but the point of the experiment was to see if we could influence you to say it was. Every other person said that they saw movement, so we're throwing out your data!" (So much for objective science!)

Before we can merge into God, each one of us will have to face a similar, final test of piercing through the darkness.

This experience stuck with me for a long time, and I drew an important lesson from it. I had no outer point of reference with which to judge, but I could sense my own relationship to the light, which told me it was steady.

There are times in the spiritual journey when we grow discouraged, or when doubts assail us. The path before us can become obscure: We may feel lost, with no light to guide us. Then the questions come: "Am I good enough to follow a path to God? Will these teachings really work for me?"

At such times, try to feel your inner relation with divine light. Though you may not be able to see it, try to sense its steady, unmoving presence within you. Those of materialistic consciousness may try to convince you that the light is no longer there where you know you saw it, or simply not there at all, but determinedly cling to its ever-present reality .

There's a beautiful story that Swami Kriyananda told us about Rajarshi Janakananda, Paramhansa Yogananda's most advanced disciple. Rajarshi was just at the point of attaining *nirbikalpa samadhi*, when suddenly everything went dark inwardly. For years during meditation he'd been seeing great light, but in an instant it all vanished.

There was a strong temptation to doubt everything he'd experienced, but he kept trying. After days of darkness, suddenly Rajarshi saw a little point of light, and gradually it came closer and closer. The light expanded until it became Master, then in turn Sri Yukteswar, Lahiri Mahasaya, and Babaji; then finally, Rajarshi merged into the Infinite.

Swamiji concluded this story by saying that before we can merge into God, each one of us will have to face a similar, final test of piercing through the darkness. And so even now, if the light seems to disappear, cling with determination and even doggedness to the truth that it is unmoving and unchanging. That light is the source of all that is. It is our truest reality, and we must eventually claim it as our own.

With joy,
NAYASWAMI DEVI

CATCHING GOD

O nce when I was young, perhaps three or four years old, my uncle was visiting our family. He had a quirky sense of humor that tended toward practical jokes. I was playing outside on a sunny spring morning, when he joined me in the backyard with a saltshaker, and a mischievous look on his face. As happens during spring in Minnesota, our yard was filled with robins hopping around looking for worms.

My uncle asked, in a conspiratorial manner, "Do you want to catch a robin?" Of course I did. What fun! He said, "Take this salt-shaker, sneak up, and put some salt on a bird's tail. Then when it turns around to taste the salt, you can catch it."

I spent quite some time trying this scheme, only to fail time and again. Finally, in frustration, I sat down in the grass. My mother, who had been watching this little drama and knowing that I had fallen victim to my uncle's tricky ways, came out, picked me up, and gave me a big hug. Then we went into the house together to have some hot cocoa.

Another time, many decades later, I was more successful in trying to catch something. This time we were at Ananda's community near Assisi, Italy, enjoying a relaxed dinner with some friends. Suddenly, one of the women screamed, "There's a mouse! There's a mouse!" Her scream, of course, frightened the poor little creature, and it scurried away. This was a situation that begged for a solution, and I had one.

I asked for a shoebox, which I propped up with a fork, and put some cheese inside. I tied a string to the fork and enjoyed the rest of the meal and a long, lovely conversation with our friends. But out of the corner of my eye, I was watching the box. Eventually, the little mouse came out and went for the cheese. I jerked the string, the box fell over him, and he was caught. A little later we took him out and let him go in the woods.

Of these two stories, I think that, oddly, the first is the better way to catch God. The second story left me feeling a certain sense of accomplishment in my trapping prowess, which drove out the realization that I never caught the mouse: It caught me. After all, with a little reflection we begin to realize that it was Divine Mother playing all the parts: the mouse; the box, string, and cheese; and all the friends sitting at the table. She was entertaining us for the evening. My little sense of pride made Her hide, just as surely as the scream of my friend had the mouse.

Sometimes we need calm, sustained determination, remaining alert for God's whispers.

But both stories illustrate a valid part of our quest to catch God. Sometimes we need calm, sustained determination, remaining alert for God's whispers. Ultimately, however, any energy we put out is only part of the picture. Yogananda said that our efforts amount to twenty-five percent, while the grace of God and Guru makes up the other seventy-five percent.

If we think we can catch God with "tricky ways," we are sadly mistaken. The first story shows us that there are things, both in this world and in our spiritual quest, that are beyond our willful control. When we try to put salt on the tail of God, He always seems to flit away. Finally, in surrender, we need to sit quietly in a pleasant, sunny place. When we do this in meditation, Divine Mother comes, wraps us in Her arms, and takes us home.

In joy,
NAYASWAMI JYOTISH

EXIT STRATEGIES

"YOU ARE HERE" is written on the poster in bold letters, next to a bright red X. A line of arrows leads from the X, showing the exit route that leads out of the building in case of a fire. Every hotel room we've ever stayed in has such a sign posted inside the door, and although I've never actually studied one carefully, it is comforting to know that it's there.

In our spiritual development, we may start to look for a different kind of exit strategy. Paramhansa Yogananda spoke of the "anguishing monotony" that comes when we realize that we've been trapped for a long time in a world where true happiness cannot be found. Then we begin to look for ways to escape suffering permanently, and for this we need more than one of those posters.

Ananda Moyi Ma
(with thanks to anandamayi.org).

The true way out is found through the guidance of God or one of His enlightened children — one who is free from delusion.

I'm reading an inspiring book now: *A Goddess Among Us*, by Swami Mangalananda, about the life of a great woman saint of the twentieth century, Ananda Moyi Ma. The book contains a story of one of Ma's young disciples, and how the saint helped her to escape the confines of this world.

24

The girl was once standing in line to receive Ma's blessings at the conclusion of a satsang. Ma's health was quite poor at that time, and her attendants had formed a tight guard around her to prevent people from touching her feet. As the disciple stood in line, she felt an intense longing to touch Ma's feet, and began mentally praying to receive this blessing.

As her turn came and she stood before Ma, she suddenly found that "time had stopped," and she was in a completely private world with Ma. There was no sound, and she saw only the saint, who extended her feet towards her. Kneeling down, the girl lovingly held Ma's feet to her head in reverence. Then, as she stood up, the noise and the attendants returned. The girl moved on, realizing that no one else had witnessed that magical moment when she'd "stolen" that sacred touch.

An even more dramatic story in this regard comes from the life of the great sixteenth-century Spanish mystic and saint, John of the Cross. Along with his elder mentor, St. Teresa of Avila, he sought to reform the Carmelite Order to its original purity, which had been lost over time.

His reform efforts were met by fierce opposition from powerful Church leaders, and in 1577 John was arrested, imprisoned, and tortured. Kept in a tiny cell, which was no more than a crawl space between two walls, he was subjected to frequent public lashings and a starvation diet. This went on for seven months.

Finally, one evening in the dead of night, a great light appeared in his cell, and Christ stood before him. The prison walls seemed to melt away, and he quietly made his escape. Though weakened and in pain from his harsh treatment, he found his way to one of St. Teresa's convents, where he was protected and nursed back to health. Later he received protection from the Pope, who gave him permission to found and lead a new monastic order.

Friends, if you feel the problems of life are closing in around you, and all your exit strategies lead to dead ends, remember to seek help from God and the great saints. Through them alone can we find the soul freedom we are seeking.

Swami Kriyananda composed a wonderful children's song whose words are:

> Nothing on earth can hold me;
> Rise, O my soul, in freedom.
> Nothing on earth can hold me;
> Rise, O my soul, in freedom.
>
> Rise, O my soul, in freedom:
> Nothing to fear anymore.
> Rise, O my soul, in freedom:
> Nothing to fear anymore.*

May your search for inner freedom be met with fulfillment.

NAYASWAMI DEVI

* crystalclarity.com/144

CELEBRATIONS

When Swami Kriyananda finished a big project—a major book or series of talks — he would usually gather a small group of friends together and take a short vacation to relax and celebrate. Devi and I were often blessed to accompany him on these celebratory trips. His favorite destination in America was Carmel, California, a picturesque former artist colony on the Pacific Ocean. Its shops, galleries, and winding streets reminded him of Europe. What wonderful memories we have of those times when he shared his joy with Divine Mother!

"The Next Wave," by Nayaswami Jyotish.

We, too, have reached a landmark that calls for a celebration. This is my 200th *Touch of Light* blog, and next week Devi will reach the same total. When we started writing them in 2013, we didn't know how long we would continue with these weekly offerings, or that they would reach so many people. We were just doing our part to share the light we had received from Paramhansa Yogananda.

Many times, the most difficult part was coming up with a fresh idea for the blog. There were instances when, facing a deadline, I stared uneasily at a blank screen. Then an idea flashed into my mind as if from outer space. I've come to recognize these inspirations as gifts from God and Gurus; my part is to be open to receiving their grace. I've learned, tentatively at first, but more and more confidently, to cooperate with their help and even count on it in sticky situations. The best part is that this has expanded beyond the blogs to all areas of my life.

God often works His magic through others. Many new ideas have come during a conversation with a friend, and I've learned to be on the lookout for these opportunities, like a bird-watcher always ready for a new sighting. It is very reassuring to recognize that Divine Mother plays with us through our friends. Ratan Tata, the founder of Tata Motors, one of India's largest corporations, said, "If you want to walk fast, walk alone. But, if you want to walk far, walk with others."

Another lesson we've learned writing these blogs is that it takes a certain amount of perseverance to go many years without ever missing a deadline. Our spiritual quest also demands endurance. Daily challenges are God's way of helping us develop the strength and perseverance we need in order to find Him. One time Swami Kriyananda said, "We can't always rely on inspiration to carry us through. Sometimes we just need to roll up our sleeves and get to work."

One of the great lessons we've learned from him is that life should be filled with joy. Work can be done joyfully, not grimly. "Energy is ours," he once wrote, "not when we hoard our strength, but when we devote it willingly, joyously toward the achievement of that in which we deeply believe."

As the Bible says, "To everything there is a season, and a time to every purpose under the heaven." There is a time to let the will-power part of our minds rest, to relax and refill the tanks. There comes a time to celebrate, enjoy some good food, a walk by the sea, and the sense of accomplishment that comes from reaching an important landmark.

Then, inevitably, there also comes a time when the next blog is due. I enjoyed a comment by Elon Musk when he was informed that he had become the world's richest person. He said, "That's weird. Well, back to work."

But now is a time for celebration. Since, due to the pandemic, we can't travel physically, we are happy to celebrate with you, our friends and family from around the world.

In joy,
NAYASWAMI JYOTISH

P.S. Our blogs have been compiled into five books so far: *Touch of Light*, *Touch of Joy*, *Touch of Love*, *Touch of Peace*, and (the book you hold in your hands) *Touch of Divine Wisdom*. — Nayaswami Jyotish and Nayaswami Devi, January 2023

MORE THAN A MOTHER

ast week Jyotish wrote that the blog "Celebrations" marked his two hundredth offering. Well, friends, here is my two hundredth, making a grand total of four hundred blogs we've posted since we started writing them in 2013. Thanks to all of you for your support.

There was another much more important event that also took place last week. On March 7 we celebrated the anniversary of Yoganandaji's *mahasamadhi*, his final conscious exit from the body, in 1952. The timing was perfect both to celebrate Master's life and to reach this milestone with our blogs, since these offerings were all done in service to him.

Swami Kriyananda wrote about Master's passing in his autobiography, *The New Path*:

> They brought Master's body to Mt. Washington and placed it lovingly on his bed. One by one we [the monastics] went in, weeping, and knelt by his bedside.

> "Mother!" cried Joseph [one of the monks]. "Oh, Mother!" Indeed, Master had been a mother to us all — ah, and how much more than a mother!

That phrase, "how much more than a mother!" kept reverberating in my mind. I began to think about how the guru expresses the mother-child human relationship, but expands it to the limitless horizons of soul communion.

What are some of the qualities of a mother that are expressed in an exalted way by the guru?

First, there is an expansion of human love into divine love. As our soul moves from lifetime to lifetime, we have different mothers who care for us in each of our many incarnations. We form bonds of love with them which then recede at the inescapable separation of death.

But each soul has only one God-ordained guru who guides us eternally through successive incarnations. His timeless message to each one, Swamiji wrote, is this: "I love you always, through endless cycles of time, unconditionally, without any desire except for *your* happiness, forever, in God." This kind of love — eternal and unchanging — is rooted in the very foundation of creation.

Another expanded quality is patience. Our human mother watches as we learn haltingly to talk, to walk, and to use our bodies. When we fall down, she picks us up and sets us back onto our feet, steadying us until we can confidently walk forward once again.

So it is with the guru, but so much more so. The guru's patience must endure over many lifetimes, as he supports our efforts to walk on the spiritual path. When we stumble, or go off in the wrong direction (as we all inevitably do), there is no judgment on his part. Patiently and with infinite care, he helps us get back on our feet to resume our journey to God.

And the guru waits. He waits until we are ready to return his love — however long it may take. Master writes in *Autobiography of a Yogi*, about meeting his guru, Swami Sri Yukteswar: "'O my own, you have come to me!' My guru uttered the words again and again in Bengali, his voice tremulous with joy. 'How many years I have waited for you!'"

The human mother also offers her child guidance about how to live in a way that brings happiness. Her instruction, however, is often limited by her own lack of deep understanding. Guidance rooted in the ego cannot bring us the fulfillment we're seeking.

The guru, by contrast, offers his wisdom and teachings based on eternal universal truths, on techniques tested over time, and on his own experience. Meditation, Kriya Yoga, right attitude — all these are offered to guide our souls toward union with God.

Rather than seeking to protect us from the consequences of our actions, the guru works with an understanding of the Law of Karma. He guides us through the suffering caused by our past mistakes, and shows us how to begin freeing ourselves from old karmic patterns.

Finally, if the guru is "more than a mother" to us, how can we be "more than a child" to the guru? In India the word for disciple is "chela," or "child": a spiritual son or daughter of the guru. Our human mother we can love, respect, and serve, but mother and child must always remain separate beings.

In the case of our guru, however, if we offer ourselves whole-heartedly with deep trust, faith, and surrender, we find that guru and chela can become one. Then the guru, who is more than a mother — more than a father, friend, or beloved — shows us that we were always one with God's infinite love and joy.

In reverence and gratitude,
NAYASWAMI DEVI

HOW TO LIVE
AUTOBIOGRAPHY OF A YOGI

For our annual Inner Renewal Week starting next week we will focus on various writings of Paramhansa Yogananda and Swami Kriyananda, including *Autobiography of a Yogi, Conversations with Yogananda,* and *The Essence of the Bhagavad Gita.* But reading and discussing books is all too often merely an intellectual exercise, even when it is inspiring. We want to take a different approach. We will take the teachings, examples, and stories of these "scriptures" as practical guides on how to live. After all, unless we integrate good advice into daily life it does little to change us. Here are a few strategic gems in the *Autobiography.*

Make the search for God a central focus of your life. Yogananda starts his great opus with this immortal sentence: "The characteristic features of Indian culture have long been a search for ultimate verities and the concomitant disciple-guru relationship." This states the theme of the book and shows us the right goal for our lives. Swami Kriyananda begins each of the vows he wrote by declaring that the spiritual search should direct our lives, and he makes the point more strongly, the deeper the level of commitment involved. In the vow of complete renunciation for nayaswamis, he expresses it this way: "From now on, I embrace as the only purpose of my life the search for God."

Expect miracles. *Autobiography of a Yogi* is filled with stories of miracles. Yogananda says that, even from birth, he had clear memories of past lives, and complete awareness. And he says it with humor: "The beguiling scope of an infant's mind! adultly considered limited to toys and toes." He is subtly giving us yet another guide for how to live: with humor, laughter, and joy.

Then he moves on to rarer occurrences, of masters who can manifest themselves in wheat fields and hotel rooms, levitate, bilocate, and be in constant conversation with Divine Mother. He convincingly follows the example of Jesus, who said, "Unless you see signs and wonders, you will not believe."

It may seem that miracles happen only to Yogananda and other great souls. Have you and I seen miracles? Yes, absolutely! If we but peer behind the curtain of outward appearances, miracles abound in our lives. Yogananda states that we couldn't live for a minute without the constant flow of grace from God. Sometimes God makes His grace more obvious. Many times on a birthday or special occasion for Swami Kriyananda I have seen a rainbow appear, sometimes in a clear blue sky. It has become a semi-expected sign of blessing at those times.

But the greatest miracle of all is the inner transformation that takes place when we make the spiritual quest a true goal of our life. One time Devi was lamenting to Swami Kriyananda that she didn't think she had made much progress. "How can you say that!" he replied forcefully. "You are a completely different person than you were when you came to Ananda." I have been blessed with a life where I see ordinary people gradually becoming transformed into saints. What greater miracle can I expect?

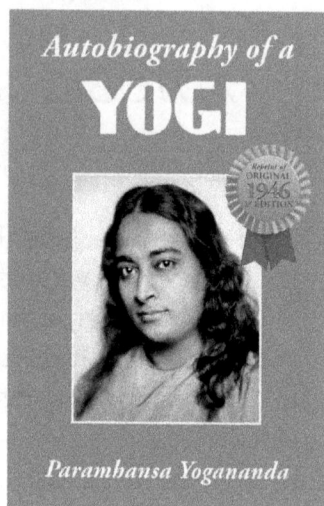

These blogs are too short to be able to discuss at length so many other themes in the *Autobiography*. But here, briefly, are a few for you to consider as guides to your life:

Fill your life with love: love of family, love for your guides, and, most importantly, love for God.

Seek to be in the presence of saints. If you don't happen to have any living in your neighborhood, as Master did, then start with books. If you are sincere, you will be led to living saints.

Meditate, pray, chant, and let the very flow of your breath be filled with a yearning for eternal verities.

I have read *Autobiography of a Yogi* many times, perhaps you have too. Now is the time to take a step beyond reading it and begin living it.

With love,
NAYASWAMI JYOTISH

AN EVENING IN THE ETERNAL CITY

oday a friend of mine sent a cartoon in which a couple are seated together in a living room, and the woman says, "One day 2020 will be a one-word catchphrase for everything messed up. 'How's your day going?' someone will ask you. 'A total 2020,' you'll answer. 'Say no more,' will be their reply."

There's probably truth behind the humor, because 2020, continuing now into 2021, has certainly been a challenge for everyone on this planet. Our lives have been changed, turned upside down, and may never return to what they were. However, there's a secret to finding peace and happiness no matter what changes or setbacks are coming your way.

I first got a hint of it one evening in Rome when we were with Swami Kriyananda. It was late, and we'd just had a long, lovely dinner at the home of a dear friend, Renata Arlini. As we were walking back to our hotel, the lights from the shops and restaurants illumined the night, there was a hint of autumn's chill in the air, and a light rain started to fall. Swamiji stopped at a street stall to buy Jyotish a much-needed umbrella.

Then we walked along in silence, when suddenly Swamiji said in a quiet voice, "How many dinners in how many homes in how many languages have I had!" As we strolled through the beautiful tree-lined avenues of Rome towards our hotel, Swamiji's few words seemed to open up a different dimension of time. Nothing outwardly changed, but somehow we were living *in the moment* — everything was clearer, crisper, as though illumined from within, and we were a part of everything. Time itself seemed to stand still.

What was different? Before, we'd been enjoying friendship, good food, and the sights of a beautiful city. We'd been taking pleasure in all these things, but we were living *for the moment*, experiencing it with some attachment to our enjoyment. Swamiji's simple statement about his life of non-attachment and self-transcendence was a secret to how to face all of life's experiences: the enjoyable, the not-so-pleasant, and the downright horrific.

Paramhansa Yogananda put it this way: "It is helpful to think of God as being forever with us: right here and right now, ever in the present tense. Ask yourself, at the same time, why are people so irresistibly drawn to living *for*, rather than *in*, the moment? In other words, to identify with the fleeting scenes and ever-fluctuating circumstances around them: changing events, endless streams of people, both enemies and friends. Unfortunately, it takes time to banish the mental hypnosis that all this, and that time itself, is a reality, focusing one on the desire for ephemeral sense-experiences."

How can we make this change to living *in*, not *for*, the moment? It's not rocket science, friend. Meditate so that you experience your own inner self. Offer your life in service to God through others. Cling not to anything or anyone, and don't identify with the "fleeting scenes and ever-fluctuating circumstances."

Then 2020 can be remembered not as the year when everything went wrong, but as an opportunity that brought you closer to true freedom and happiness. Be part of a group that says, "It was a total 2020," and means, "It was wonderful."

With joy,
NAYASWAMI DEVI

THY WILL BE DONE

Today is the anniversary of the crucifixion of Jesus, one of the three central events in Christianity. Anyone who grew up as a Christian is intimately familiar with the image of Christ dying on the cross. Easter, of course, represents the resurrection and the triumph of life over death, of spirit over body.

There are many aspects to these events, but I want to talk about one in particular that is essential to spiritual progress: the deep surrender of the individual will (ego) to the divine will. Amidst the drama of the arrest, trial, crucifixion, and resurrection, it is easy to overlook this timeless teaching, but true spiritual progress is impossible without self-offering.

The Bible tells us that Jesus was betrayed by his disciple, Judas. Jesus, being omniscient, knew what was coming. He prayed, "O my Father, if it be possible, let this cup pass from me: nevertheless not as I will, but as thou wilt." When the soldiers came to arrest him, Jesus said, "Thinkest thou that I cannot now pray to my Father, and he shall presently give me more than twelve legions of angels?"

There is a deep lesson here for all of us. No matter what comes to us, good or bad, we should willingly offer ourselves into God's will. In the case of Jesus, this surrender allowed him to alleviate the karma of the entire world, and especially of his close disciples. Our lives may be less dramatic and earthshaking, but surrender to God's will is the best way to neutralize the karma

Michelangelo's Pietà (housed in St. Peter's Basilica at the Vatican).

that keeps us bound in delusion. Acceptance of God's will is demonstrated by all great masters. Here are two fascinating examples.

One time Lahiri Mahasaya, walking back from a bath in the Ganges with a disciple, asked him to tear off a strip of cloth from his dhoti. The confused disciple didn't heed his master's request. A block or so later a brick fell from a roof and struck Lahiri on the foot, causing a gash which bled profusely. Lahiri calmly tore a piece of cloth from his own robe and bandaged his foot. The astonished devotee asked, "If you knew that was going to happen, why didn't you simply avoid it?" Lahiri responded, "The karma needed to take place, and if I had avoided this, it would have had to come back later in an even stronger form." A wise teaching for us when we are thrashing around trying to escape a karmic lesson.

Paramhansa Yogananda had many organizational responsibilities even though he yearned to spend more time in complete communion with God. One time he prayed to Divine Mother to be relieved of all those onerous tasks. Her response is both humorous and instructive. He heard Her voice saying, "I have to take care of the whole universe. Can't you look after one little corner of it for Me?" What else could he do but roll up his sleeves and get back to work?

So in order to find ultimate fulfillment, we all must attune our individual will with God's will. If Jesus had tried to avoid the cross, he might have had a happier ending to his personal story, but there would have been no crucifixion, no resurrection, and very probably, no Christianity.

In surrender to His will,

NAYASWAMI JYOTISH

WITHOUT A DOUBT

was once visiting a friend who had recently given birth to her second child, a lovely little girl. Her first child, a precocious three-year-old named Tamara, was exhibiting definite signs of jealousy towards this newcomer with whom she had to share her parents' attention.

As my friend lovingly cradled the sleeping infant in her arms, Tamara approached with a knowing look in her eyes and asked, "Mommy, is that baby icky?"

"Oh, no," was my friend's reply, "she's very nice."

Attempting to plant seeds of doubt in her mother's mind, she left with the words, "You never know."

I've sometimes wondered if Tamara grew up to be a reporter, since raising doubt in people's minds seems to be the *modus operandi* of the news today. Elected officials, spiritual leaders, health experts, sports figures: no one is immune from having questions raised about their integrity or their hidden agenda. Sometimes the headlines stoop so low as not even to pretend to have backup facts, but simply ask a question: "Is it true that Martians are living inside Mt. Everest?"

The insidious thing about being fed a regular diet of such information is that it continually activates doubt, which is a state of consciousness. Over time it becomes a chronic condition that has little to do with any particular issue, but leads to uncertainty, anxiety, and loss of faith in anything.

Paramhansa Yogananda called doubt "suicidal." He said that constructive doubt, which questions only in order to arrive at the truth, is all right, but that destructive doubt is a habitual state that eventually paralyzes the will. He went on to say, "Doubt is a mental insanity by which you absolutely refuse to recognize your own ability to cognize the world around you and to understand everything."

What can we do to rise above chronic doubt and reclaim our ability to know what is real and true? It's good to limit the time we spend looking at news or social media. Even the positive content that's shared online can take us away from our center if we give it too much focus. True knowing does not come from avoiding negative input; nor, for that matter, from seeking positive input: Its source is not the mind or intellect, but rather a sense of deep inner awareness.

Swami Kriyananda had a remarkable ability to see past people's outer personas, and to understand who they really were. This enabled him to help others and to bring out the best in them. His understanding came not from knowing facts about a person, but from being fully centered in himself and relating to that center in others. This ability is born of meditation and of having achieved deep inner stillness.

Yoganandaji said, "With a strong lens the sun's rays, focused through it, can ignite wood. Yoga practice, similarly, so concentrates the mind that the curtain of doubt and uncertainty is burned away, and the light of inner truth becomes manifest."

With that burning away of doubt, faith emerges. And with faith dawns the realization of God's presence in our lives and in everything. Once our faith is strong, no negative innuendos or aspersions can convince us otherwise. We know what we know because we feel it in every fiber of our being.

In *The New Path*, Swami Kriyananda writes: "I believe that the time is approaching when countless men and women will no more think of doubting God than they doubt the air they breathe. For God is not dead. It is man only who dies to all that is wonderful in life when he limits himself to worldly acquisitions and to advancing himself in worldly eyes, but overlooks those spiritual realities which are the foundation of all that he truly *is*."

What is this approaching time of which Swamiji speaks? It is a new dawn, when people seek and find their answers within through meditation and prayer. Only thus can we clear away the fog of doubt which obscures our ability to know truth. Faith, indeed, is the proof of things unseen, and it is through the eyes of the soul that we can see the divine truth hidden in everything.

Your friend in God,
NAYASWAMI DEVI

RELAX AND FEEL

One of the most difficult concepts for most people to grasp is that we don't so much *achieve* Self-realization as we *relax* into it. We are constantly bombarded with the message that success depends upon making a strenuous effort. While this is often true for worldly success, it is the opposite for spiritual attainment. One time Swami Kriyananda, a little frustrated with the pace of his spiritual progress, asked Paramhansa Yogananda, "Am I not trying hard enough?" Yogananda replied, "You're trying too hard. You are using too much willpower. It becomes nervous. Just be relaxed and natural."

What this means for those of us who meditate is that our success will depend upon releasing, not acquiring. Ultimately we need to release those feelings and thoughts that strengthen the ego, and simply sink into our true soul-nature.

Joyful relaxation is often the better path even in worldly pursuits. When Devi and I were starting Ananda's first large ashram in San Francisco we enjoyed running and participated in the city's famous "Bay to Breakers" race. In a park near us there was a Saturday runner's clinic open to anyone who wanted to attend. The instructor, who had been a famous college track coach, told an illuminating story about his career change.

He said, "As a college coach, I had several world-class, Olympic-level athletes on the team. Then one day a group of lady librarians from the college asked if I could coach them. Eventually, giving in to their persistence, I told them to run around the track with a moderate effort. They were thrilled with their success and over the next few weeks, as they continued to ask my advice, a nice bond formed between us.

"Then I recognized something that changed the course of my life. The librarians were always happy, positive, and having fun. My world-class runners, on the other hand, were usually upset and angry about something. Perhaps they had been edged out in a race or failed to set a personal best by a tenth of a second. One day a light bulb went off in my brain — I realized that I was coaching the wrong type of people. I ended up quitting my job and the stress that went with it. Now, I coach runners who just want to have fun, and my life also has become fun."

Our meditations should be more like fun-runs than competitions. When we simply watch the breath and relax, the life-force withdraws naturally. Swami Kriyananda has defined meditation as "listening." The only effort we should make is to focus and relax. Our concentration should be intense, but not tense. If we do that, God will take care of the rest. It may take time to overcome past tendencies and karma, but in the end, if we are sincere in our desire for God, He must respond.

Yogananda said, "Don't feel badly if you find yourself too restless to meditate deeply. Calmness will come in time, if you practice regularly. Just never accept the thought that meditation is not for you. Remember, calmness is your eternal, true nature."

With joy,
NAYASWAMI JYOTISH

A LETTER TO SWAMI KRIYANANDA

Today is the anniversary of Swamiji's Moksha Day in 2013 — when he discarded the worn-out garment of his body and found soul freedom. Rather than write *about* him, I thought I'd write a letter *to* him and share it with you.

April 21, 2021

Dear Swamiji,

This morning we had a beautiful meditation in your apartment at Crystal Hermitage to honor your passing eight years ago. I love spending time there, because it brings back such sweet memories of shared moments; of places we traveled together with you; and of the profound divine wisdom and love you shared with everyone.

As we sat quietly in the blessing of your presence, of the joyful freedom of your consciousness, I was reminded of the loving friendship in God that you gave equally to all. As you once said to me (really as a correction for needing personal attention from you), "Remember, no one is special to me. I'm not even special to myself."

In the years since your passing, many devotees you never met in person have told us of the huge impact that you've had on their lives. As we continue to witness your ability to inspire others including us, and to guide the growth of Ananda, we realize over and again how well you kept your true spiritual stature hidden. Only a great soul would have been able to achieve what you did and still do.

Yet for all your depth of realization and breadth of accomplishments in serving Master, you never lost the ability to make everyone feel that you were their dearest friend. I remember David Hoogendyk (one of your first students when you starting teaching in San Francisco prior to Ananda) saying shyly to me towards the end of your time on earth, "All these years I've hardly ever spoken to Swamiji, but he is my best friend."

There was a beautiful statement made about Ananda Moyi Ma regarding the "paradox of omnipresence." It was said that she made one feel the closest of dear friends, and yet she remained wrapped in an aura of inaccessibility. As time goes by, I realize that you always seemed so accessible, friendly, interested in our problems, yet part of you was always very far away, resting in Master's omnipresent spirit.

So thank you, dear divine friend, for taking us as little children on the spiritual path and teaching us to walk with our own strength; to serve and realize our own potential to help others; and to speak the language of love to God and Guru.

I know that you're already aware of how well the Ananda communities and centers are doing, even in the midst of the current pandemic. You spent years preparing us: making us aware that, as Master had forewarned, the world would be facing very hard times.

Now that such times are upon us, we haven't been taken by surprise, and consequently are able to meet with strength the challenges before us. You showed us the need to prepare not only in practical terms, but, more importantly, mentally and spiritually, so that now we can help others to deal with the difficulties confronting us all.

You said more than once towards the end of your sojourn on earth, "I no longer know where Swami Kriyananda ends and Master begins." This transformation became apparent to those around you as you seemed increasingly like a small wavelet resting on the calm surface of Master's oceanic consciousness. It was beautiful to behold the drop of your individuality slipping into the ocean of bliss.

Swamiji, I could go on writing about how you changed our life, the lives of countless others, and indeed the world, but better to commune with you inwardly in meditation. You have been sorely missed, yet your presence has never been lacking. Again the paradox of both your individuality and universality.

From time to time I allow myself to think of the joy it will be when we greet you again in a realm of light. Until then, though the veil of separation remains, it grows thinner. Thank you, dear Swamiji. You have given our life meaning and purpose, and taught us how to realize our true potential: the infinite joy of God.

Your loving child always,

devi

I hope that you enjoyed this letter from my heart. May we all move towards moksha and find the joy that is our destiny.

NAYASWAMI DEVI

YOUNG BODIES, OLD SOULS

We had a lovely dinner on the lawn with a group of friends last week, the first in more than a year. As the conversation deepened over the evening, we asked each person to talk about what they were working on inwardly. Their answers probably resonate with you too: "I'm working on staying in the moment." Another, "I'm working on being spiritually authentic to myself rather than doing what others might expect." Yet another, "I'm trying to keep my mind God-centered throughout the whole day." One said, "When I have a question, I try to remember to ask God or Master, 'What would you do?'" Around the table it went, each sharing deeply their inner aspirations and struggles.

What made this remarkable is that we were sitting with a group of younger people, some of whom had been here for only months. The age of our bodies doesn't matter; what counts is the "age" of our souls. These were all old souls in young bodies.

What is an "old soul"? In one way, this is a misnomer: Our souls have been around since the beginning of time. But in another sense, an old soul is someone who has spent a number of lifetimes pursuing spiritual truths. Anyone drawn to a high and challenging spiritual path such as that given by our great line of masters has to be an old soul.

Once we were with Swami Kriyananda in, of all places, a shopping mall when he said, "I received a letter yesterday from someone expressing how unworthy he felt about himself. He compared his accomplishments to mine and felt inadequate. I wish," Swamiji went on, "that people would understand that we are all the same. I've just been at it for a little longer."

An important point here is that there are many deep aspirants who are struggling with unhelpful self-images. Many feel alone and without support from their environment. Most old souls, many in young bodies, experience feelings similar to the ones below:

- "There is so much more to life than what I see happening around me. I am not attracted to the things that others find so important. This world doesn't seem to fit me."

- "I wish I had friends I could talk to, who feel as I do. But I feel alone. I don't have anyone that I can share myself with, who really understands my deeper feelings."

- "I want to help the world." (This may take a thousand forms: helping the homeless, or the environment, or those who are unable to defend themselves from those with more power.)

- "I feel that I am spiritual but not religious. I wish I could find someone who can explain the purpose of life."

These were some of the feelings being expressed at the table last week. What was notable was that everyone felt secure enough to bare their souls. These young people had been a part of our Internship Program at Ananda Village, and now were moving toward living here permanently. The Internship Program gives young people a chance to stay here for a period of time without any long-term commitment, to see if Ananda seems to be the right path and environment for them.

Whether young or old, it is a deep blessing to find a safe and supportive environment in which to allow one's spiritual aspirations to unfold. Yogananda said that environment is stronger than willpower, and urged the creation of "world brotherhood colonies" based on simple living and high thinking.

The world is desperately in need of social models that help people live lives of higher meaning and purpose. What Ananda is offering globally are such examples. Master's great mission to the world has hardly begun.

NAYASWAMI JYOTISH

P.S.: Here is a link to Ananda's Virtual Community: crystalclarity.com/131.

FACING GRIEF AND LOSS

The pandemic in India has created a situation that is both heartbreaking in terms of human suffering and staggering in its numbers. Many reputable sources say that the reported statistics of 400,000 new cases of Covid and 3,000 deaths per day are actually many times lower than the true figures.

Yet what really brings this situation home for me are the letters and texts from our friends in India. This morning we received one from Ananda's center leader in Bangalore, in which she wrote: "The situation here is astonishing. Almost every member of our community has a friend, relative, coworker, or someone else close to them who either has Covid, is recovering in the hospital, or has passed on."

And from an Ananda group leader in Mumbai: "Today we did another Astral Ascension Ceremony. . . . Fifteen more deaths within our Ananda family and friends since last Sunday."

Even as we grieve for and with our friends, I think we all are asking, "Why is this happening?" One can point to mistakes made by political leaders and to the dire consequences of poverty and overpopulation, but we should also look for deeper reasons behind what's occurring on the surface.

Swami Kriyananda has said that India is the guru of the world. Through their search for ultimate truth, India's sages down through the centuries have given us the science of yoga, the model of the guru-disciple relationship, and the Vedantic philosophy in all its depth.

Now is the time for people everywhere to reflect on India's teachings that this material world, which seems so real, is only *maya*, delusion. The light of God's consciousness, from which our souls have been brought forth, is the only true, lasting reality.

In the Bhagavad Gita, when Arjuna grieves for those who will die in the impending battle, Krishna consoles him with these beautiful words:

> With words of love (and seeming wisdom) you have been grieving over those who deserve no lamentation. The wise mourn neither for those who live on earth nor for those who leave it. . . .
>
> The indwelling Self is ever changeless, imperishable, and without limitation. Only these fleshly garments can be destroyed. . . .
>
> That Self is not born, nor does it perish. Self-existent, it continues its existence forever. It is birthless, eternal, changeless, and ever the same.

In Paramhansa Yogananda's *Autobiography of a Yogi*, we read in page after page about the unreality of death. In thrilling stories he tells of the physical resurrection after death of his guru, Sri Yukteswar, and in turn of his guru, Lahiri Mahasaya. The first of this spiritual lineage, Babaji, is a deathless master who has chosen to remain in a physical body for this cycle of time to guide and uplift humanity.

Master also relates there his own unusual vision regarding death. While in Kolkata at his father's home, Yoganandaji was sadly reflecting on the vast toll of death occurring on the battlefields of Europe during World War I. Suddenly he found his consciousness transported to the body of the commander of a battleship under siege. A bullet pierced his chest, and he fell dead.

"At last the mysterious footstep of Death has caught up with me," he thought. Suddenly he found himself once more seated in lotus posture at the home in Kolkata. Joyfully, he realized he was alive in a body free of wounds. No sooner had he begun rejoicing, however, when to his bewilderment he once again found himself in the body of the dead captain.

"Lord," he prayed, "am I dead or alive?"

A dazzling light filled the horizon. The words came forth: "What has life or death to do with Light? In the image of My Light I have made you. The relativities of life and death belong to the cosmic dream. Behold your dreamless being! Awake, my child, awake!"

What consolation can those of us find who have lost loved ones? Of course, we will grieve for them as Master did as a young boy when his mother died. But beyond that loss is the promise that our souls will be united forever in God.

Yoganandaji wrote a beautiful prose-poem entitled "Conquering Fear of Death: The Dying Youth's Divine Reply." It tells of a beloved youth who is mortally ill. His family sobs, begging him to stay, but he replies joyously, "You weep for me dark tears, sorrowing at your impending loss in me, but I weep for you glad, joyous tears, for I am going before you — yes, for your own welfare's sake also — to light candles of wisdom all the way. I shall wait for you there, to welcome you to my place of eternal freedom with my one and only Beloved, and yours."

So, my friends, why is this happening? Perhaps to remind us that God's light and love are the only realities is this world of shadows. The suffering of the pandemic will pass, but grief and suffering will come again wearing another garb. The only lasting way out is to dissolve into God's light.

Let us draw comfort from His eternal reassurance. It will give us strength to serve others in need. As my friend from Bangalore wrote in her letter, "This situation has brought so many people together from all over India. It is the spirituality and depth of India that are shining forth during this time of horror. Everyone is helping in some way, big or small. People everywhere are stepping up and being selfless and creative in helping their country."

With loving thoughts and prayers,
NAYASWAMI DEVI

THANK YOU, SWAMIJI

S wami Kriyananda was the sculptor who chiseled my heart and soul. My life has been transformed by trying to live according to his example. His birthday is May 19, and it seems fitting, as a kind of birthday present, to thank him for some of the ways he changed me and countless others.

Divine Friendship. Swamiji usually signed his letters, "In divine friendship." For him, this wasn't just a phrase, but a living reality. He embraced everyone in an aura of acceptance. The day I met him, Easter Sunday in 1967, I arrived uninvited at his door in San Francisco along with my brother-in-law. He and a small group of friends had plans to go to Golden Gate Park for a picnic. He could easily have told us that he was busy and sent us on our way. In fact almost everyone else I've ever known would have done just that. But not Swamiji. He greeted us with delightful enthusiasm (another of his characteristics) and invited us in to join the group.

If, at that critical moment, he hadn't enfolded me in his divine friendship, my life would probably have taken a completely different course—I shudder even to think of what meandering road it might have followed. Thank you, Swamiji, for inviting me into your life, and thank you for your friendship. It has been my constant support and guide, especially in times of trial.

Living Wisely. Swamiji exemplified Yogananda's teachings of "simple living and high thinking." I read a beautiful quote from Ananda Moyi Ma that captured Swamiji's life. "To a human being, the most noble, irreproachable line of conduct should alone be acceptable. It is a matter of great rejoicing if anyone strives to mold his life upon this pattern. Only actions that kindle man's divine nature are worthy of the name of action; all the rest are non-actions — a waste of energy." Swamiji didn't waste much energy.

Even in times of relaxation, his life-force moved in an upward direction. We often joined him with a small group to watch his favorite movie, *Bambi*. He liked it, not so much for the story, but for the lovely music, the beautiful colors, and most of all for the charming, innocent friendships among the creatures of the forest. It was, for him, a depiction of divine friendship in nature. When the movie ended and we walked home, it was always with a happier, more open heart. Thank you, Swamiji, for showing me how to uplift my heart and mind.

Leadership. Swamiji was an amazing leader and accomplished a great work for Master because of it. While there were many aspects to his leadership, they might be boiled down to two principles. 1) Don't let leadership be an ego game. 2) The job of a leader is to bring out the highest and best in others.

In our various leadership roles over the years, Devi and I would meet regularly with Swamiji. He would listen sensitively and guide us. When Ananda started the work in Italy, that first winter was very cold and very difficult. When Swamiji visited a few months later, we told him about the many difficulties we had faced. Rather than commiserate with us he said simply, "No great work is ever started without someone's tapasya (self-sacrifice)." Swamiji always wanted us to think about others, not our own problems. That precept—not thinking about yourself—is one of the great keys to a successful and happy life. Thank you, Swamiji, for helping me to avoid the pitfall of self-focus.

Discipleship. The very core of Swamiji's life was his discipleship to Master, and a continual love offering to his guru. He strived to let all of his words, thoughts, feelings, and actions be guided by Yogananda. Toward the end of his life he would say, "I don't know any longer where Yogananda ends and Kriyananda begins." I pray that I, too, will be able to say the same when I am ready to exit the stage. Thank you, Swamiji, for your discipleship, and for the purity of your life. And thank you for taking on the task of sculpting my life and those of so many others.

In divine friendship,
NAYASWAMI JYOTISH

WHAT GOD GIVES . . .

T here is a powerful story from the life of Paramhansa Yogananda about the importance of rising above our likes and dislikes. It took place at a special ceremony at which he gave a lady student a red rose to wear. "But I don't *want* a red rose," she protested. "I want a pink one." The Master answered her strongly, "What *I* give, *you* take."

Paraphrasing Master's words, Swami Kriyananda wrote to us in 1976 just after the forest fire had destroyed all of our homes at Ananda Village. "I was so touched by everyone's spirit. It is admirable, and certainly pleasing to God. I believe many blessings will flow from it, and from this trying experience. I was particularly sad for you, Devi, to be given such a test so soon after having your baby. [Our home was destroyed eleven days after our son was born.] But then, what God gives, we take. He has His own program for our spiritual growth."

What God gives, we take. Living with full acceptance of this truth frees us from the downward spiral of ego-centered self-interest born of our likes and dislikes. The sage Patanjali, in his *Yoga Sutras*, offers this classic definition of yoga, or union: "*Yogas chitta vritti nirodha*"—Yoga is the neutralization of the waves of feeling.

The limited ego is constantly telling us, "I want this, not that: this situation, not that; this outcome, not that; this person, not that." Reacting to life according to our likes and dislikes keeps us forever bound to the delusion that things in the material world have the ability to make us happy or sad.

"Twenty-Nine Palms," by Nayaswami Jyotish.

But when, through meditation, we begin to still these ego-born feelings, a new realization dawns on us: We are now, and have always been, part of a much greater reality: God's unconditioned joy. Our awareness of this has been limited only by our infatuation with limitation.

Look at the suffering in the world around us now, and perhaps in your own life. Rather than pushing difficulties away, or angrily shaking your fist at an indifferent God, try to see everything as coming from a loving Divine Mother for your spiritual growth. Every test, if met with the right attitude, becomes a blessing to draw us closer to God.

Here are two suggestions that can help you overcome the tendency to act according to your likes and dislikes. First, when you are given a choice about a course of action, don't ask yourself, "What do I want?" but rather, "What do You want, God?" If you have the courage and self-honesty to follow through from an expanded perspective, you'll find yourself making very different choices that ultimately work out for the better.

Second, when difficult situations arise over which you have no control, don't bemoan your fate, or try to avoid the problem.

Inwardly accept that the test has come from God, and ask, "What should I learn from this? Where is the hidden blessing?"

After the forest fire at Ananda Village, I came to see the blessing in losing everything we had: the realization that my security didn't come from outward things, but from God's presence in my life. From that understanding came a strength and peace that have remained with me through many tests over the years.

To quote again from Swamiji's letter: "If we place ourselves unreservedly in God's hands, He proves to us abundantly how unfailing His love is for us."

With joy in God and Guru,
NAYASWAMI DEVI

ENERGY FLOW IS THE KEY

'd like to share an illustrative little story someone sent us:

A young man who was receiving training from his guru was going about his duties, and the guru noticed he seemed a little depressed. The guru asked, "My boy, why are you so sad?" And the young man replied, "Sir, I love hearing you speak about the Bhagavad Gita. But the problem is I don't remember much afterwards. It just goes in one ear and out the other. The other boys easily talk about the holy teachings, and yet I know nothing. I really wonder if I'm worthy of being here."

The guru was thoughtful for a moment. Then he asked the boy to bring the coal basket, and the boy ran quickly to the stove and brought it back. The inside of the basket was completely covered with black coal dust. The master said to him, "Fill that basket with water from the river and bring it back to me." When the boy looked befuddled, the master said, "Don't be worried. Just do as I say."

So the boy dipped the basket into the river, but before he could get back to the guru all the water had leaked out. The guru said, "Do it again."

Five times the boy went to the river and filled the basket with water. Each time he ran faster and faster in an effort to get back while there was still some water in the basket, but it was always empty by the time he returned.

Finally the boy said, "Teacher, you have given me an impossible task! It's useless to try to bring you water in this leaky thing." And the guru said, "You think it is useless? Look inside the basket." The young man looked and saw that the basket was now completely clean. The water had washed away every trace of coal.

And the master explained to him: "You may not remember or understand everything when we study the Bhagavad Gita and talk about these holy teachings. But just letting the teachings flow through you will gradually change your consciousness until your heart is cleansed of delusion and darkness."

Then the master put his arm lovingly around the young disciple and said, "Just remember: God is not a scholar, God is a lover. And if you seek Him sincerely, one day you will see how He has changed you utterly."

In many ways this story illustrates the spiritual transformation that happens through the flow of divine energy. If we get behind the outer-shell appearances to the underlying energy we can move mountains. Here are a few examples:

In meditation: When your mind gets distracted or restless, it is useless to try to think your way out of the predicament. Try, instead, to relax, breathe calmly, and visualize a steady flow of light from the heart to the spiritual eye. As the energy flow becomes calm and focused your mind will follow.

With money: Money is simply a means of exchanging your previous labor for something you want. See it, then, not as something valuable in itself, but as a flow of energy. If you do, you will be much more effective in drawing the resources you need. It will also ease a lot of worry.

Relationships: When talking or working with someone, try to feel that you're exchanging your energy with them. For effective communication Swami Kriyananda suggested the following: Try to feel the energy in your heart. Then project it through your spiritual eye. Feel their response in your heart. It will make normal conversations much sweeter and difficult ones much easier.

During this age of energy, we will be much more effective in everything we do if we can feel the energy underlying the form or the action. And if we can feel as well that it is always Divine Mother's energy that flows through us, we will end up shiny clean like that coal basket.

With joy,
NAYASWAMI JYOTISH

WATCH FOR THE "AHA" MOMENTS

Over the years I've learned a lot about life by observing parents shopping with their children. Once in a supermarket I watched a little girl who was noisily demanding of her mother some goodie she wanted. After trying repeatedly to placate her child with noncommittal answers, the mother finally blurted out in exasperation, "The answer is maybe, and that's final!" This kind of answer has proved very useful to me over time.

I witnessed another drama at a different grocery store: this time at Master's Market at Ananda Village. Shortly before the dinner hour, a mother had brought her young son along as she shopped for some items for the evening meal. The boy, a quiet, thoughtful child, saw an array of chocolate bars and cookies on the counter and asked his mother if he could have one.

"Not before dinner, dear. It will spoil your appetite."

Her simple reply brought a profound change in him, and his eyes began to look distant and sad. It was as though he were remembering many such occasions, perhaps from other lifetimes, in which his expectations for happiness from material things were thwarted. Looking earnestly at his mother, he said, "Mommy, I don't want to be in this world anymore."

Quickly doing a complete turnaround, his mother replied, "Here, why don't you have two candy bars?" But the "aha" moment had already happened. The cords of his attachment to this world had begun to fray.

Those "aha" moments are the portals through which deeper insights come to us and change our lives. Watch for them, for example, when you're trying to make a decision about which course of action to follow. Usually we approach such decisions rationally, weighing the pros and cons. Once in a while, we have an "aha" moment in which we can see the ultimate outcome of each choice. Then we know confidently which road to follow.

Watch for such moments also in understanding others. There is a tendency in human nature to categorize people and put them in boxes — whether it's a person we've known for a long time, or someone we've just met. Sometimes, however, we'll have an "aha" moment when we see a certain look in their eyes, or hear something they've said almost to themselves, and we can see who that person really is. Hold on to this deeper understanding and your friendships will continue to grow and blossom over time.

In meditation, it's especially important to watch for these moments of awakening. From time to time, we may find ourselves plodding along in our spiritual efforts, but not having the breakthroughs that take us to a deeper level. Then, one day, as Yoganandaji put it, "From behind the clouds of drudgery of routine meditative habits, there burst upon my consciousness the aurora of bliss."

When these moments come, and they will, don't let the experience fly away like dry leaves in autumn. Emblazon it on your mind. Try to return to that state of consciousness in meditation as often as you can. The intensity of the "aha" moment may fade over time, but if you inwardly cling to it, you will never lose it entirely.

Finally, watch for those magical moments in seeking God's presence in your daily life. A friend of mine was sitting in a secluded garden at Crystal Hermitage on a quiet, windless day, and was silently sending her love to God. Suddenly, without a hint of breeze, the wind chimes hanging in a nearby tree began playing one of Yoganandaji's chants, "I am the bubble, make me the sea." At first she thought she had just imagined it, but when after a few minutes it happened again, she knew that God was listening and responding.

If we continue to look for God's presence around us, we may be surprised to realize—AHA—that He was always there. Master has written a beautiful prayer-demand: "O Father, may I behold Thee: above, beneath, behind, around—wherever I turn my gaze! Train the children of my senses never to stray from Thee, who dwellest at the heart of everything. Turn my eyes inward, to Thy changeless beauty. Attune my ears to silence, that I may hear Thy subtlest music. Breathe on me the heavenly scent of Thy sacred presence."

When the veils of delusion part, we will realize that these "aha" moments are not random occurrences. They are God's way of lovingly answering His children's demands and guiding us forward through life.

With joy and blessings,
NAYASWAMI DEVI

WHEN TIME IS SHORT

We sometimes find ourselves in a situation in which we simply don't have as long for our meditation as we would like. When this happens, the solution is not to skip our practice, but to do a shorter sadhana with greater intensity. In a short meditation it is especially important to make an effort to concentrate deeply.

This principle of intensity works on the physical level too. A friend of ours recently recommended a book about exercise, called *P.A.C.E.*, by Dr. Al Sears. Dr. Sears begins the book with many scientific studies showing that short, intense periods of exercise are remarkably beneficial. We actually build greater lung volume (an important indicator of health), stronger muscles and bones, and improved cardiovascular capacity by exercising intensely for 12 to 20 minutes than with longer, more moderate efforts. The essence of his system is simple. Do brief periods of increasingly intense activity spaced apart by recovery periods. Any type of exercise that causes you to get out of breath will do. Be sure to build up gradually, especially if you aren't starting out in good physical shape.

When time is short, we can apply the same principle of intensity to meditation. On those days it is helpful to include other spiritual practices during the rest of your day. Swami Kriyananda used to tell a charming story about this.

There was a devotee who never missed his three-hour morning meditation. This, of course, vexed the Devil, who decided he had

When time is short, apply the principle of intensity to meditation.

to take action. He told his assistant devil, "Tomorrow make sure the man oversleeps so that he doesn't have time to meditate."

After having carried out this scheme, the assistant asked the Devil if he wanted him to do the same the following morning. "No," the Devil said with a sigh. "Tomorrow, make sure to wake him up on time so that he can do his usual meditation."

"But, why?" asked the perplexed imp.

The Devil replied, "Normally, after meditation that man just goes about his business. But, today, he spent the whole day thinking about God and apologizing to Him. I would rather have him meditate for three hours and then forget God than have him think about Him all day long." Swami always had a great laugh over this story.

One way to think about God throughout the day is to take a simple chant and let it repeat in the back of your mind. Periodically, when you can, give it your full concentration. I have been doing this lately by inwardly chanting "Jai Guru" and "AUM Guru," which is what Swami Kriyananda told me to repeat after I had asked him if I should take a mantra.*

* You can watch my brief description at **crystalclarity.com/132**.

Of course, we shouldn't make a practice of short meditations. It is important that we give our spiritual search priority and make time for it. Unlike physical exercise, we won't exhaust ourselves by longer spiritual efforts. As Paramhansa Yogananda said in his great mystical poem, *"Samadhi,"* "By deeper, longer, thirsty, guru-given meditation comes this celestial *samadhi.*"

I'll end with one of my favorite prayer-demands from Paramhansa Yogananda's book, *Whispers from Eternity*: "O Divine Sculptor, Chisel Thou My Life":

> Every sound that I make, let it have the vibration of Thy voice. Every thought that I think, let it be saturated with the consciousness of Thy presence.

> Let every feeling that I have glow with Thy love. Let every act of my will be impregnated with Thy divine vitality. Let every thought, every expression, every ambition, be ornamented by Thee.

> O Divine Sculptor, chisel Thou my life according to Thy design!

In joyful devotion,
NAYASWAMI JYOTISH

ATTITUDES FOR A BETTER WORLD

S wami Kriyananda has written a visionary book called, *Hope for a Better World! The Small Communities Solution*. In it he shows how the materialistic attitudes of society today have brought us to the present state of worldwide tension and suffering. He also describes how global peace and happiness can be achieved through the spread of spiritual communities.

"Is it realistic," he writes, "to hope for peace and harmony in this world? Yes, of course it is, if one's hopes are kept *realistic*. Peace and harmony must be sought first on a small scale, not in grandiose schemes of world betterment. The important thing, always, is that people be allowed to develop *as individuals*."

Though Swamiji shows how communities are the solution for the social ills that plague us today, we know that not everyone has the opportunity or desire to live in them. People everywhere, how-ever, can practice the underlying attitudes that have been at the heart of Ananda's success for more than fifty years. This success can be measured in terms both of the upliftment it has brought to the world as a whole and of the true happiness of those indi-viduals who live by these basic principles. Here are some of them that we all can apply in our daily lives.

Working with Energy and Fluidity

The hallmark of the new age in which we live — Dwapara Yuga — is a vision of the world as consisting not of fixed, separate forms but of fluid, unifying energy. In creating Ananda Swamiji put out tremendous power, but with the understanding that energy has its own intelligence. To succeed in any project, he didn't ask, "How have others done this before?" or even, "How have I done this before?" He tried to think in new ways as guided by the dynamic energy now awakening in the world.

Much of the conflict we find around us is between the forces of change and the fear of losing the status quo. By attuning with this flow of universal energy, you'll be amazed at the new, cre-ative solutions that emerge to guide you forward in any situation.

Seeing the Unity in Diversity

Behind the diversity of nations, cultures, and religions there is one divine consciousness: God. The more we see past the su-perficial differences that divide us, the more we perceive people's underlying unity. Yoganandaji therefore called his intentional communities "world brotherhood colonies."

One of the greatest gifts of living in a community is to accept and respect others whose perspectives may be very different from your own — and to cooperate with them. This can be done by trying to see the common thread in seemingly opposing points of view.

When people cooperate in this way, each individual gains an expanded perspective that shows a higher purpose to even mundane activities. Much of Swamiji's success came because he supported the ideas and growth of everyone.

Living in Simplicity

Another of Yoganandaji's main tenets for community life was "plain living and high thinking." When we begin to break the dependency on material things for our happiness, we find inner freedom and Self-sufficiency.

You may know the story of our experience of living through the forest fire in 1976 that destroyed most of the homes and structures at Ananda Village. Our son was ten days old when we lost our home and all of our possessions.

At first, I must admit, I was in a state of shock, but the maternal instinct then quickly asserted itself. I realized that the sense of home and security that I wanted for our child was not dependent on outer things, but had to spring first from my own heart. No loss of possessions could diminish the love and nurturing that I would give to our son. This was an incredibly freeing and life-transforming experience — it has shaped my life ever since.

Developing Strength AND Flexibility

Everyone's life has its share of challenges. In watching Swami Kriyananda build Ananda, I saw that he had perhaps more than his fair share. Strength is needed to deal with one's difficulties, but not the rigid type that we see in weight lifters who move about like stiff robots.

Strength needs to be balanced with flexibility, of the kind we see in hatha yogis. A number of times over the years, Swami Kriyananda would put out tremendous effort to accomplish some goal in building Ananda. But if he came to feel that this was no longer the right course, he would turn on a dime and redirect his efforts towards a different end. He adapted to what was needed at any given time, and wasn't afraid to look foolish for changing his mind.

Faith and Self-Offering

God is ultimately in charge of everything we do and everything that befalls us. By trusting in His loving presence, communities and individuals can weather many a storm. The more your faith is tested and validated, the more you can offer yourself unreservedly to God and Guru.

Yoganandaji has a beautiful prayer-demand: "O Spirit, teach me to pray and worship incessantly, with deepest concentration. O Spirit, balance my meditation with devotion, and purify my devotion with all-surrendering love unto Thee."

Meditation, devotion, self-offering — these ultimately are the bedrock upon which communities are built, and upon which we can build our lives in God.

Joining hands and heart with you in this great adventure,
NAYASWAMI DEVI

GOD'S HIDDEN LANGUAGE

One of the most thrilling episodes in Paramhansa Yogananda's *Autobiography of a Yogi* is when Sri Yukteswar, after his death, materializes in front of Yogananda. Yogananda writes, "For the first time in my life I did not kneel at his feet in greeting but instantly advanced to gather him hungrily in my arms." Then a little later, "My mind was now in such perfect attunement with my guru's that he was conveying his word-pictures to me partly by speech and partly by thought-transference. I was thus quickly receiving his idea-tabloids."

We have the delusion that words, written or spoken, are the only means of communication. In fact, the vast majority of communication is nonverbal. Only a moment of reflection will suffice: If God has manifested as everything, then there is an underlying connectedness and communication between everything. This goes all the way down to the subatomic quantum energies.

I have been reading a fascinating book, *The Man Who Listens to Horses*, by Monty Roberts. Through careful observation of wild horses, he discovered their hidden language. Using the old, rather brutal, method of breaking a horse, it takes around two weeks to finally break its will sufficiently for it to carry a rider. By understanding the hidden language of horses, Monty is able to accomplish this in a half hour. And the horse, instead of fearing him, works enthusiastically in partnership with him. As proof of concept, not only has he "joined up"—as he calls it, rather than "breaking"—with thousands of horses, but he has also won innumerable championships in the equine world.

It is only the arrogance of ego that makes us think that we, with our human language, are unique in our ability to communicate. As our awareness continues to advance during Dwapara Yuga, increasingly we will see the interconnectedness between all things. Articles are appearing weekly that share the latest discoveries by scientists of the communications among plants, ants, animals, and atoms.

Language may allow more detailed communication, but it is vastly inferior to the type of exchange that Yogananda described. As a sidenote, Gene Roddenberry, the creator of *Star Trek*, took many of his ideas from *Autobiography of a Yogi*. He said that the image of the transporter came from Sri Yukteswar's dematerialization, and I suspect that the Vulcan mind meld came from the same chapter.

If we want to speak with Divine Mother, we need to learn Her hidden language. We should take our first hint from the title of a book that Yogananda called scripture — *Whispers from Eternity*. God speaks quietly, and only a quieted mind can hear the divine whispers. So we must strive for deep stillness in meditation. Secondly, feeling is more important than intellect when trying to receive God's communications, so we must open our heart center through deep devotion in order to hear His whispered vibrations. Finally, the real communication happens not only behind the curtain of words, but also behind restlessness of thought. In deep inner stillness and devotion the innate intuitive perceptions of the soul will begin to be heard.

Let us take a lesson from Monty Roberts and learn a new language, not of horses, but of Spirit. When we do, Divine Mother will speak to us tenderly in the same way She did to Yogananda: "Always have I loved thee! Ever shall I love thee!"

In divine friendship,
NAYASWAMI JYOTISH

PLANNING FOR YOUR NEXT INCARNATION

The little boy was orphaned at an early age when both of his parents were killed in a tragic accident. Fortunately, he was taken in by his loving grandparents, who raised him in the tradition of his people: the Cherokee. Thus begins *The Education of Little Tree*, a beautiful book which describes the ways of these indigenous people, and their reverence for the Great Spirit and for all of creation.

As the boy grew to maturity, he was trained by his grandparents in both practical and spiritual skills. Then the time came when his elderly grandmother knew her life was coming to an end. As was the Cherokee tradition, in her final moments she looked into her husband's eyes and said, "Next time it will be better."

No regrets, no apologies, no clinging to what was, but simply the assurance that all souls are forever joined in spirit and are evolving towards higher consciousness.

This practice reflects the wisdom of the Indian masters, who tell us that life is a school to teach us the lessons our soul needs to find freedom. We move from incarnation to incarnation until we realize who and what we really are. Yoganandaji described the soul's journey as an ascent up "the spiral stairway of wakefulness."

What can we do to prepare for our next incarnation? First, look at the unfulfilled desires and ambitions to which you're clinging.

Ask yourself, "Do I really want these? Will they bring me lasting happiness?" If the answers are "yes," then put out the energy to achieve them, and move on. If not, work to weed out their roots, which can entangle your consciousness.

Introspect and look at the negative mental or physical habits that hold you back. It takes honesty, persistence, and energy to overcome these, but with determined effort you can change any aspect of your life.

Don't identify with your faults, but understand that these are just reflections of actions you performed in the past. They are karmic patterns you yourself set in motion, that now you can change. As Sri Yukteswar said, "Everything in future will improve if you are making a spiritual effort now."

The ideal is to do your best, and to remain objective and non-attached. Every challenge you face in life is a lesson placed there for one purpose: to teach you something you must learn in order to find freedom. Don't waste time on things that are empty distractions and ultimately slow your spiritual progress.

It's important also not to dwell on past mistakes or failures. Keep affirming the virtues you want to develop, and take these goals forward into your next life. Once Swami Kriyananda was asked by his guru, Yoganandaji, to be in attendance at the deathbed of one of the Master's students, a dignified man and a retired architect. In the last moments of his life he muttered remorsefully, "I've done many bad things in my life."

Afterwards Swamiji came to Master and recounted what had happened. Yoganandaji replied, "He shouldn't have said that. He will take this attitude of regret and guilt into his next incarnation." Master went on to say that even if you are dying of a terrible disease, if you can affirm, "I am well" at the end, you will take that thought into your next life and have a healthy body.

So, how do we plan for our next incarnation? Right now take stock of your life: Eliminate what's holding you back, and strengthen, or at least affirm, what will take you forward. Ask God to show you the soul lessons you need in this life, so you can quickly learn them. Always live in the thought that inner freedom is very near.

If you do these things, you may be surprised to find that your present life, too, is transformed. There may indeed be no compulsion to reincarnate at all. As Yoganandaji said, "When your schooling is done, and the end comes, and people are crying at your passing, you can rejoice and say, 'Beloved One, Master Death is opening for me the gate to freedom. I have had enough schooling now. I shall go out no more.'"

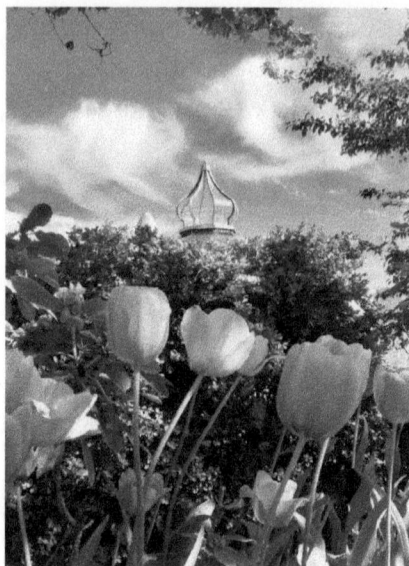

In the distance, Moksha Mandir, Swami Kriyananda's final resting place, at Crystal Hermitage. "Moksha" means final soul liberation.

With joy and freedom,
NAYASWAMI DEVI

FAITH, ATTUNEMENT, AND COURAGE

We just received news that a friend in India, Ashok Baba Kulkarni, is close to leaving his body. We've considered him a friend and an inspiration even though we met him and his wife, Daya, only a few times. On every occasion, he would regale us with stories of his time with his guru, Ananda Moyi Ma. Ashok Baba didn't have a big public mission, but for me he represents India's truest treasure: those deeply spiritual souls who carry the light of God and illuminate the world around them as they pass through.

A few years ago he told us a fascinating story that has deeply inspired and instructed us. He and his wife were very close to Ma, and she would often ask them to accompany her on her travels. One time a small group was staying in a very remote area. It fell to Ashok to do the daily shopping, no small feat, since it required a walk of ten kilometers to the nearest small village, and a return trip carrying the purchases, which along with his other tasks took him all day.

As a part of his sadhana, Ma had instructed him to do a large number of repetitions of a sacred mantra. My memory is that it was 108 malas' worth, which is nearly 12,000 daily repetitions. One day Ma asked him if he was doing his mantra, and he replied that he was constantly repeating it as he walked to and from the market.

Her reply surprised him. She said, "No, this is not good enough.

You should repeat them during meditation instead, so that you can concentrate deeply." Another member of the group came to his defense, saying, "But Ma, that would take him all night." Ma just shrugged and said nothing more.

That evening when he came back to his little hut he told his wife, Durga, about the conversation and said, "Let's start tomorrow night." Her reply (a rebuke to the procrastinator in all of us) was, "Why wait, we must start tonight." And so that night, they did their meditation and mantra and went without sleep. The next night they did the same, now going without sleep for two days. And so it continued for a whole month.

Ashok concluded the story by saying, "It was a true miracle. We never slept for an entire month and yet were filled with energy and joy. I would never have believed such a thing was possible if I hadn't experienced it myself."

Ashok Baba Kulkarni, disciple of Ananda Moyi Ma.

As I reflected on this story, I was struck by the faith and courage it must have taken. I could imagine myself following my guru's request the first night. But think about the second and third nights: that must have required a special kind of faith and courage. Their attunement alone had to sustain them until they were able actually to experience their guru's grace sustaining their efforts.

I pray that Ashok's life will be an inspiration for all of us to develop that kind of faith and courage. May it help us take a step beyond what we think of as our limits. As we do this, we will expand toward our soul-nature, which never sleeps and has no boundaries.

In God's light,
NAYASWAMI JYOTISH

P.S. As I write this, it is four days before the blog will be published. Today, our daily calendar of passages from *Autobiography of a Yogi* quoted a passage that I took as Yogananda's blessing. Describing his first meeting with Ananda Moyi Ma, Yogananda wrote, "I had instantly seen that the saint was in a high state of *samadhi*. Utterly oblivious to her outward garb as a woman, she knew herself as the changeless soul; from that plane she was joyously greeting another devotee of God." I suspect she is now preparing to greet her beloved disciple, Ashok.

IS FREEDOM FROM KARMA POSSIBLE?

Recently we were discussing the law of karma with a few friends. One of them made an interesting comment that karma doesn't always come back immediately, but hangs around for a while. It isn't, he said, as if there were a credit card company keeping track of charges and payments each month. That's why we need a "Master Card" to help us work through our karma over many lives.

The "Master Card" is, of course, the guru: God's agent acting in this world to guide each soul to freedom. A disciple of Paramhansa Yogananda told us of an interesting dream he once had. In it, he was walking along a beach with a child's plastic pail and shovel in his hand. He suddenly came upon a huge mound of tarlike black material, and he knew that this was his past karma that he must remove to be free. He began laboriously to chip away at the

"*Shores of Cosmic Peace*," by *Nayaswami Jyotish.*

sticky mound, filling his little pail only halfway after much effort.

He persisted at the task, when, almost at the point of giving up in despair, he heard a loud racket coming from the other side of the tremendous pile before him. Quickly running to see what

86

was making the noise, he saw Paramhansa Yogananda riding on a backhoe with a huge bucket, joyfully scooping up vast quantities of the "tar-ma" and throwing it into the sea.

By our own efforts, the task of removing our past karma seems nearly impossible. Still, we must earnestly do our part. A discouraged disciple once said to Master that working out all our karma seemed hopeless, that "one might as well try calming the waves on the ocean."

Yoganandaji answered: "It is a big job, I grant you. Still, it isn't nearly so difficult as it looks. For, ask yourself this: What is it that causes the waves to rise and fall in the first place? It's the wind. Without wind, the surface grows calm automatically. Similarly, when the storm of delusion abates in the mind, the waves of action and reaction subside automatically. So what you must do is still the waves of your mind by deep meditation, and then, in meditation, rid yourself of the consciousness of ego-involvement."

When Yogananda said that the wind is what keeps the waves crashing, he was referring to the breath. In the Bhagavad Gita, Arjuna says to Krishna that the mind is restless and more difficult to control than the wind. Krishna replies that it can be controlled by yoga practice and mental dispassion. The deeper meaning of this passage, as Yogananda explains, is that by calming the breath through pranayama and meditation, we gain control over our mind, and can transcend ego-identification. Then the seeds of our karma cannot find soil in which to take root in our consciousness.

Here is a technique for using the breath to overcome past karma:

1. Inhale deeply and concentrate all your energy at the point between the eyebrows.

2. Feel that you are burning away faults, bad habits,

negative thoughts or tendencies—fruits, all, of your past karma.

3. Exhale completely and keep your breath out as long as you can comfortably. Feel completely free within yourself.

4. When you breathe in again, think of a positive image or memory, and let it fill your mind.

5. Repeat this several times in a row. Practice this daily until you feel a release from some karmic burden.

Yogananda also counseled that by acting without desire for the fruits of our action, we will gradually be freed from the bondage of karma. To act is necessary. But, "During activity, never feel that it is you who are acting. Act, instead, with the thought that God is the Doer. . . . Desireless action is the pathway to freedom."

This is one of the main themes of the Bhagavad Gita, in which Krishna tells a reluctant Arjuna that he must fight the impending battle of good against evil. He goes on to explain that by selfless action we are playing our part in this world and fulfilling our destiny. "Therefore, strive conscientiously during the performance of all actions, whether physical or spiritual, to act without attachment. By activity without self-interest, one attains the Supreme." (3:19)

The grace of the Guru; meditation and breath control; action without attachment to the results: These are the keys to overcoming karma. Yoganandaji showed us these ways in which we can remove the mound of our past karma and open the doors to soul freedom.

Your friend in God,
NAYASWAMI DEVI

I CAN CHOOSE

In 1937 Yogananda wrote to his most advanced disciple, Rajarshi Janakananda, "I used to come home, my hair saturated with smoke and my eyes burning after luncheon talks. I felt even suffocated. One day I made up my mind, Divine Spirit was smoke and light, and I was never bothered since. Mind is everything, whichever way you train it."

Mind is everything. What a powerful truth! It is almost as if the entire spiritual path can be reduced to this concept: The essential spiritual battle is to see that fulfillment lies within, rather than by changing outside conditions.

The world of the senses and maya (illusion) constantly tries to trick us into focusing outward, on things and circumstances. This is the lesson of the famous gambling scene in the great epic, the *Mahabharata*. Yudhisthira, who represents discrimination, and Shakuni, who represents material attachment, play a game of dice in which Yudhisthira loses his kingdom. With every roll of the dice, Shakuni proclaims, "Lo, I have won!" Of course he wins. He cheats! We, too, gamble with delusion, but delusion always wins. As Yogananda put it, One thing you can be certain of is that delusion never keeps it promises.

"Mind is everything, whichever way you train it." With a puff of smoke, Yogananda gives us a universal solution to the problems in our lives.

So how can we train ourselves to be happy regardless of circumstances? Here are several ways that have worked for me, although you may well have other strategies that work for you.

We can train ourselves to be happy regardless of circumstances.

1. **Reframe the problem.** Yogananda couldn't change those smokey rooms, so he reframed the problem. He realized that smoke was not the real difficulty, but rather his seeing smoke as something other than Divine Spirit. As soon as he reframed the problem as one of perception rather than conditions, the battle was won.

2. **Practice our techniques.** There are many techniques that can help us choose to be happy in spite of what is happening. In tense moments, we can gain control of the mind by controlling our breath through regular breathing. We can use affirmations to help us turn our thoughts and reactions in a positive direction. We can focus our energy powerfully at the spiritual eye. For those who know them, both the Energization Exercises and Kriya are very powerful, even life-changing.

3. Shift to the here and now. Many problems, such as worry, judgment, or disappointment, exist only in the mind. By focusing in the present we can stop these mental tapes from cycling through their incessant repetitions.

4. Divert the mind. The first step toward reversing negative reactions is to introduce a positive flow of energy. Sometimes, the best short-term solution is just to do something fun. Take a walk in nature, have a good laugh, paint, cook, dance, or sing. It doesn't matter what you do, only that you enjoy it. During enjoyment, you forget yourself and your problems for a little while.

The most important thing of all is to realize, *I can choose!* I can choose to be happy in all circumstances. I can choose to be loving regardless of how I am treated. I can choose to be calm and peaceful no matter what storms howl around me.

Joy, love, peace, calmness are all different aspects of the Divine. By choosing these, we choose to swim in the sea of Divine Spirit. Then, as Yogananda said in his great poem, "*Samadhi*":

A tiny bubble of laughter, I
Am become the Sea of Mirth Itself.

In joy,
NAYASWAMI JYOTISH

OUR OWN POSSIBILITIES

All of life is bound together by a common purpose. From the lowliest worm to the most exalted saint, all are seeking the same goal: bliss. This search may take many forms—from finding a juicy leaf to union with God—but this shared desire for true happiness motivates us all.

People do themselves a disservice when they put great saints on a high pedestal beyond their own attainment. The masters are not different from us in *kind*, but in *degree* of awareness. They're our spiritual parents who have walked before us on the path to bliss, and they've come to show us how we, too, can get there.

"Babaji & Christ," by Nayaswami Jyotish.

In *Autobiography of a Yogi*, Paramhansa Yogananda writes of the deathless Himalayan master, Babaji: "Only one reason, therefore, can motivate Babaji in maintaining his physical form from century to century: the desire to furnish humanity with a concrete example of its own possibilities."

Our own possibilities: this is what we should bear in mind when we become discouraged about our spiritual progress. Swami Kriyananda once told us about a letter he'd received from someone who was downhearted that while Swamiji had done so much in his life, he himself had been able to accomplish so little. Swamiji was quiet for a while, then added strongly, "He shouldn't feel that way about himself. He needs to understand that I've just been at it longer."

By putting saints in a special category, we blind ourselves to the fact that they, too, have had tests and flaws that they've overcome by perseverance. Remember that the great ones have stood on the exact spot where we stand now. With determination and hard work, however, they've surmounted the obstacles that stood between them and bliss.

In Swami Kriyananda's autobiography, *The New Path*, he tells this story from Yoganandaji's life: "Bernard [one of the monks], upon whom Master had been urging some difficult undertaking, remonstrated one day, 'Well, Sir, *you* can do it. You're a *master.*'

"'And what do you think *made* me a master?' the Guru demanded. 'It was by *doing*! Don't cling to the thought of weakness, if your desire is to become strong.'"

If we face our tests with confidence and strength, these same challenges become our greatest tools for spiritual growth. Then we can see our limited human consciousness not as a barrier, but as a bridge to divine accomplishments.

This, then, is the gift of the great souls who have walked before us on the spiritual journey: They show us that we, too, can find the bliss we're seeking. They have given us techniques, tools, right attitudes, as well as their examples of courage and strength to guide us on.

In Swami Kriyananda's play, *The Jewel in the Lotus*, one of the characters is a saintly sadhu wandering in the Himalayas, who tells a small group of his followers: "A true guru comes to this earth, not to show people how different he is from them, but to inspire them with a sense of their own divinity."

We are one with all life in our shared quest for bliss. We are one with the great masters in our shared innate divinity. It is up to us now to claim these inherent aspects of our being as our own, and finally to reach the end of our soul's journey.

With joy,
NAYASWAMI DEVI

THREE QUESTIONS

What is working? What isn't working? What if?

A delightful painting instructor uses these three questions as part of his artistic process. When he is making a sketch for a new painting, he looks at his first attempt and keeps those things that are working, changes those that aren't, and asks "What if I did this instead?" He repeats the process again and again until the painting is finally finished.

There are some interesting qualities to these three questions. First, they work at all scales. You can ask them about a small sketch, and you can ask them about society as a whole. They work equally well at both the atomic and the cosmic scale.

It is more effective, however, to focus on those areas you can actually change. A sketch you can change. A national issue, not so much. You can avoid a lot of emotional upset and stress by not fretting about those things over which you have absolutely no control.

Another quality of these three questions is that they can be applied to any area of our lives, from the most mundane to the highest spiritual realms. Here are a few thoughts on how we can do that.

Physical: Start with our environment. Due to habit, inertia, or lack of awareness, we often live with things that are less than ideal, even problematic. Take five minutes to do this exercise.

Look at the room you are in as you read this, and ask these three questions: What's working?, what isn't?, and what if? Maybe you need to throw a few things into the trashcan, or move a piece of furniture, or remove something that doesn't belong in the room. If it is quick, do it now. Then make a "to do" list for bigger things that can be improved. Later on, take some time to apply the same process not only to other rooms in your house, but also to your diet, exercise, sleep, and other aspects of life on the physical plane.

Mental/Emotional: We can get into habitual patterns of thinking and reacting that pull us down. Our mental/emotional environment can be approached in the same way as our physical space. Think about your patterns especially in those areas that are painful or difficult, and ask yourself the three questions. Some habits and attitudes should be thrown into the trashcan, others removed from your present mental space and put on a shelf to work on later. Remember, you want to work on things *you* can change, rather than on how others need to transform themselves.

Spiritual. Look at those things you can improve, such as meditation habits, use of techniques, attitudes, and devotion. Realize, however, that spiritual progress occurs on many levels and in its own timing.

You might end up with quite a few things you want to change, but don't try to act on them all at once or you will diminish your enthusiasm. The canvas of your life is a big project. One thing that I've learned with painting is to take on only one small area at a time. I can't change everything at once even on a small canvas.

It is also very important to keep things in perspective and celebrate all the things that *are* working. Change is all part of the process. Enjoy it!

Paramhansa Yogananda has written, "Self-analysis is the greatest method of progress. Without it man becomes a living machine.

Every tomorrow is determined by every today. Did you ever count your faculties or measure their strength?" Swami Kriyananda suggests, "Every night before sleep, review the day to see how you did on the battlefield of life."

Try doing this with the three questions, "What worked? What didn't? What if?" Step-by-step you will improve until your canvas is finished and you can put it in a frame and give it to God.

With love and joy,
NAYASWAMI JYOTISH

YOU CAN GET THERE FROM HERE

There's a joke I enjoy sharing about a traveler who found himself lost in an unfamiliar countryside. Luckily, he spied an old farmer standing by the side of the road surveying his fields.

Approaching the old man, the lost traveler asked, "Excuse me. Do you know the way to Smartsville?"

The laconic farmer paused for a while, and then replied, "Well, when ya come to the fork in the road, turn left. . . . Nope, that won't work." He started again, "Continue on straight until ya come to the bridge. . . . Nope, that won't work either."

Finally, shrugging his shoulders, he concluded, "Ya know, ya can't get there from here."

This little story actually has some interesting spiritual implications. Recently we had a satsang with friends in India on the theme "How to Find More Joy in Daily Life." As I thought about the topic, I realized that this was a contradiction in terms. You can't find *more* joy in daily life, because there really isn't *any* true joy to be found there.

*"I Am Always with You,"
by Nayaswami Jyotish.*

The sages of all religions tell us that this world isn't real in and of itself. It's God's dream, *maya*, or delusion, created by the interplay of dualities: light and shadow, joy and sorrow, pain and pleasure, birth and death.

To try to find joy in this ever-shifting world is like trying to freeze in time the movements of a bird's flight. The constant is change. One day everything will be going well for you, and you think that will last forever. The next day, however, everything changes for the worse, and you don't understand what happened.

In truth, it has to be this way, because in the end the alternating waves of duality balance out to zero. This is the nature of daily life. So to look for true, lasting happiness in outer experiences is an impossible task: "Ya' can't get there from here."

But this is not to say that life is hopelessly devoid of any fulfillment or joy. Quite the contrary! The message of the spiritual masters of all religions is one of hope, and much more: It's a promise that God's joy is the only reality, and that it can and must be found within one's self.

The secret is to seek joy not *in* our daily life, but *through* it. In other words, try to see the hidden presence of God beneath the endless waves of changing experiences. During the good times, try to feel God's joy shining beneath the surface; during difficulties, see God's smile encouraging you onward.

Paramhansa Yogananda put it so beautifully in one of his prayer-demands from *Whispers from Eternity*: "O Father, behold me through the pores of the sky. Smile at me through the twinkling stars. Strengthen me through the sun; calm my feelings through the moon. Caress me through the breeze. Love me through my love. Throb in me through my heart. Breathe Thine immortality through this mortal frame of mine. Speak through my voice. Help others through my hands. Use my mind to inspire them. Breathe through my breath. For within this fragile viol Thou alone canst sing Thy complete, eternal song."

God is the ever-new joy we are seeking through all of life's experiences. Unlike the old farmer, true spiritual teachers show us the path to find Him, and tell us: "You *can* get there from here."

With joy,
NAYASWAMI DEVI

THE PARABLE OF THE FRIGHTENED BOY

There was a young boy who lived in a small village. One night he woke up screaming, and when his parents rushed in to see what was wrong, the trembling boy said, "I was in the forest at the edge of the village just as it was starting to get dark. A huge tiger came out of the trees and began stalking me. As he came closer and closer, all I could see were his yellow eyes, so I screamed to frighten him away, and then you woke me up."

The parents reassured him that it was only a nightmare, and that there was no real tiger. But the next night the boy had the same dream and again woke up screaming. This continued every night for a week. The parents, now at their wits' end, took the boy to see their guru. The wise guru, hearing the boy's dream, didn't belittle him or tell him not to be frightened.

The guru said, "You are remembering a past life when this tiger was real. But in this life he is only a memory." He told the parents, "Each night fill a lamp with oil and place it in his room." To the boy he said, "The tiger won't come as long as the light is burning." After that, the scary dream stopped and never returned.

Although the nightmares stopped, the boy still had many fears. He was afraid of the dark, afraid of being left alone in the house, and fearful of strangers. He and his parents visited the guru as often as possible and, through his support, the fears gradually faded. But the boy still kept his lamp burning throughout the night, lest the fearful tiger return.

As the boy grew into a man, he was less fearful, but he was very shy. He learned to cope with this by staying alone most of the time and starting his own business, making artistic lamps.

As often as he could, he visited the guru, who became his anchor and support through all the storms of life, and practiced his techniques. Inevitably, as time passed, the wise teacher grew old. Then, during a cold winter night, the dreaded word came that the guru's end was near. The mature man, still a little boy in front of his guru, knelt at his feet sobbing.

The guru lifted him up and embraced him gently. Very softly he said, "I have loved you as my very own son. We have been together in many past lives and our love will draw us together again."

"But how can I carry on without you?" the man moaned.

The guru said, "Let me tell you a secret. You have never needed the lamp. I gave it to you as a crutch to help you overcome your fears. The true light is within you." Then the guru touched him at his spiritual eye, and the blaze of light in his forehead was like the sun.

"You have never truly required my support or counsel, but I gave them freely because you needed to feel my love, so that your

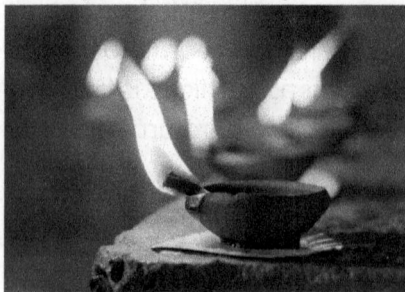

own could grow within you." Then he touched him over the heart and an immeasurable love blossomed within his chest.

"Let me now tell you a final truth. If you want this light and love to continue to burn within you, you must give them away to others. Find those who are frightened and give them light. Find someone who is troubled and surround them with your comfort. The more you give these away, the stronger and purer they will become."

The next day at the ceremony for the guru's passing, all were weeping but one. One of them—formerly shy and afraid—moved from person to person, embracing each one in turn and easing their pain. And as they looked into his eyes, it seemed to them that they were seeing only the eyes of their guru, only the rays of Divine Mother's love.

In light and love,
NAYASWAMI JYOTISH

THREE UNEXPECTED GIFTS

S ometimes the best gifts come in unexpected packages. Perhaps this is God's way of encouraging us to see the hidden treasure lying beneath the challenges in life. Here are three such gifts that at first glance seem to come in very odd wrappings: solitude, silence, and spiritual hunger.

First, **the Gift of Solitude**. Most people are either uncomfortable or bored unless others are around. If, however, we patiently see through the seeming isolation of solitude, we may find a surprising hidden reward.

There's a story of a guru who made an unusual request of three of his disciples. "I'm going to give each of you a banana," he said, "but don't eat it until you are absolutely sure that no one is watching and you are alone. Come back when you have completed this task, and tell me what happened."

Eager to please their guru, the three quickly headed off to fulfill his request. The first one returned shortly and reported, "I ran to my house, went into my room, and locked the door. Sure that no one was watching, I ate my banana, and here I am." The guru patted him on the head, and said, "Very good. Now let's wait for the others."

The next man returned after an hour. "Master," he said eagerly, "knowing that there are always people around in my home and in the shops, I headed towards the outskirts of town near the jungle. Here I was confident that I was alone, and I ate my banana."

Again the guru patted this disciple on the head, and said, "Very good. Let's wait for the last one to return."

They waited and waited, until day turned to dusk, and dusk to evening. Finally as the first rays of dawn began to creep into the sky, the third disciple appeared, looking very weary and downcast, and still holding her banana.

"I'm sorry, Master," she said. "I have failed you. I walked and walked until I found myself in the jungle. But everywhere I went, I felt that I was never alone. Deeper and deeper I went, but always I felt that someone was watching me. Because I always felt a presence near me, I couldn't eat the banana." She threw herself at her guru's feet and began to cry.

Raising her up, he said with great tenderness, "My child, you are the only one who has passed my test. You have discovered that we are never alone. The unseen Presence you felt was God, who is always with each of us."

Next, **the Gift of Silence**. How rare in the world is real quiet! The sound waves of our planet are filled with noise, because people seem to need the distraction of it. Once we had the great blessing of hearing a talk given by Richard Wurmbrand, a Lutheran priest who'd been imprisoned and tortured by the Communist regime for preaching in his native Romania. He told of being kept in solitary confinement for years in an underground cell completely devoid of light or sound. Food would be slipped in through a slot in the door once a day.

As he told of the inhuman treatment to which he had been subjected, his face became more and more illumined, until he became radiant, all but translucent. With an inward smile on his lips and a distant look in his eyes, he said, "In that absolute darkness and silence, there is the most beautiful sound."

The gift he had been given in that silent prison cell was the sound of AUM, the divine vibration from which all creation is made. In

Christian terminology, it is called the Holy Ghost, or the "Great Comforter," because it brings with it the living reassurance that we are all one with the Spirit of God.

"Mountain Glen," by Nayaswami Jyotish.

Finally, **the Gift of Spiritual Hunger**. Once a fellow disciple of Swami Kriyananda was bemoaning the fact that he didn't seem to be making any spiritual progress. He said to their guru, Paramhansa Yogananda, "Sir, I don't believe that I have very good karma."

"Remember this," the Master replied with deep earnestness, "it takes very, *very*, VERY good karma even to *want* to know God!"

Spiritual hunger, the seemingly unrequited love for the Divine, is the greatest gift of all. It is a treasure planted in our hearts by God Himself to draw us to Him. Yes, that love seems unrequited, but it is we, not God, who are holding back. With every pang of devotional yearning, with every feeling of discouragement at your progress, feel that the silent, ever-present voice of God is calling you back to your home in Him.

This treasure trove of divine gifts is ours for the finding, if we but open our hearts and minds to the hidden realities that are shining within us, around us, and everywhere.

In divine friendship,
NAYASWAMI DEVI

HAVE A LITTLE FAITH

"Have a little faith" is an expression often used in a light way, perhaps by those who are trying to prove themselves to you. But in fact, true faith is the bedrock of both spiritual success and the ability to withstand the storms and trials of life.

How many times do we despair when we encounter difficulties? Often we are faced with a choice: worry and anxiety on one hand, or acceptance and faith on the other. Faith is especially important when facing situations — like a pandemic or political conflict — over which we have no control.

There is a fascinating passage in *Autobiography of a Yogi*: "[Babaji] is in constant communion with Christ; together they send out vibrations of redemption, and have planned the spiritual technique of salvation for this age. The work of these two fully-illumined masters — one with the body, and one without it — is to inspire the nations to forsake suicidal wars, race hatreds, religious sectarianism, and the boomerang-evils of materialism. Babaji is well aware of the trend of modern times, especially of the influence and complexities of Western civilization, and realizes the necessity of spreading the self-liberations of yoga equally in the West and in the East."

This world is in the hands of God and the great ones, and we suffer needlessly when we forget this. One time, as Swami Kriyananda was preparing to leave India, one of the leaders asked him, "How can we carry on without you?" His reply was both profound and comforting, something we can all keep in mind: "Remember, this work is not your work. It is not my work. It is the work of Babaji and Master."

One time some disciples begged Ananda Moyi Ma to do something to alleviate the turmoil and suffering caused by the partition that followed Indian independence. After a long period of meditation, Ma said simply, "Don't you think that He who created this world knows how to run it?"

Patanjali said that faith is a foremost pathway to Self-realization. Swami Kriyananda further explains that "faith means far more than belief. . . . Belief on the spiritual path is important, for without it one will not even follow the path. Faith, however, depends on results; the greater the results, the greater the faith. As success in any scientific effort demands also devotion to the goal, so, the greater the faith, the greater also the devotion (in this case, to the goal of oneness with God)."

Ask Master and Divine Mother to strengthen your faith, and you will add their limitless power to your own.

How do we develop faith? Here are three things that will help:

1. Accept that it will take time and effort for your belief to mature into the kind of successful results that produce faith. We are all works in progress.

2. Include God and Gurus in this effort. Ask Master and Divine Mother to strengthen your faith, and you will add their limitless power to you own.

3. Offer all your problems and anxieties, your hopes and dreams, at the feet of Divine Mother. Do this especially toward the end of your meditation. Feel that you are not a separate entity, but just a drop in the ocean of all that is.

A recent psychological study concluded that there is one single best way to stop anxiety in its tracks. It suggests that, whenever the mind starts to worry, one should repeat a simple key word or short phrase, rather like a mantra. Something like, "relax" or "be calm." I suggest that we add another to the list: "Have a little faith."

In the Divine,
NAYASWAMI JYOTISH

RELAX UPWARD

read a true story recently about a woman who was tending her son in the hospital following a long, difficult surgery. Three days after the procedure, the boy was still in a great deal of pain, and the worried mother was unable to sleep. As she paced the empty hospital corridors alone at three in the morning, tears of worry and concern ran down her cheeks.

Suddenly she heard a kindly voice ask her, "What's the matter?" The woman was taken by surprise, since she hadn't seen or heard anyone approaching. Turning, she saw an old janitor mopping the floor. He exuded such kindness and calmness that she found herself telling him all her troubles.

"I can feel your faith," he said, "and this story has ripples, like a stone thrown in the water. Know that this is all part of God's plan."

He gave her a gentle pat on the shoulder and continued his mopping along the corridor. Suddenly, she felt a wave of calmness and reassurance sweep over her. Returning to her son's room, she was finally able to get some sleep. When dawn came, the boy's pain was almost gone.

She wanted to thank the janitor for his kindness, but when she tried to contact him, the hospital records showed that no one on the staff matched his description. In her hour of need, God's loving hand had intervened to bring her comfort.

Last week Jyotish called his blog, "Have a Little Faith." There's another way of saying this. Swami Kriyananda wrote: "*Relax upward*, toward the spiritual eye in the forehead."

When you're faced with a challenging situation, instead of getting tense and tied up in knots, try to step back from the problem. Allow your energy to flow calmly upward to the spiritual eye. Let your awareness rest there, and trust that you are surrounded and protected by God's light. In *Autobiography of a Yogi*, Lahiri Mahasaya says, "Attune yourself to the active inner Guidance; the Divine Voice has the answer to every dilemma of life."

Perhaps you've had a difficult encounter with another person. Instead of reacting emotionally and exchanging angry words, inwardly withdraw for a moment and take a few deep breaths. Become aware of the energy in your heart center, and let it flow upward toward the spiritual eye. Feel that you are relating from that point in you to that point in the other person. Once this process begins, you'll discover the way to restore harmony.

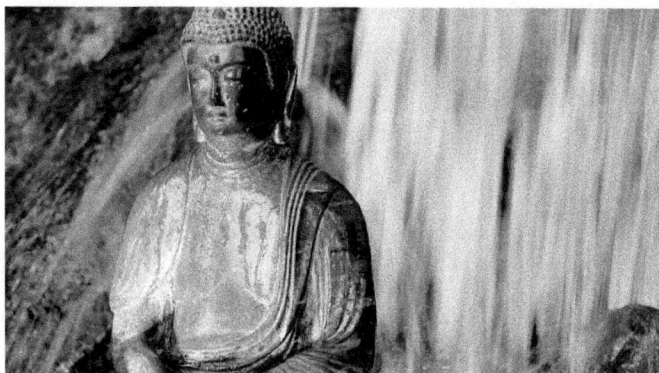

When circumstances of any kind produce stress or anxiety, don't be pulled into the downward spiral of worry and fear. Remember what the divine messenger told the woman in the hospital: "Know that this is all part of God's plan." Relax upward, and offer everything to God. Trust that whatever happens is part of that plan.

Consciously create moments of tranquility and upward relaxation throughout the day. Try to build a fortress of peace around you during the quiet times in your life. Then when the enemy attacks with its soldiers of fear and worry, you can overcome them. Over time you'll find that the bulwarks of your inner calmness and strength can withstand any assault.

Finally, and most importantly, learn to relax upward in meditation. When you sit to meditate, consciously relax: first release the tensions in the body; then the preoccupations of the mind; then the emotional involvements of the heart; and finally, any remaining blocks to which the ego clings. Release these entrapped pools of energy into a flowing current that moves upward in the spine to the spiritual eye. "Don't," as Swamiji wrote, "try to *force* your concentration to that point. Think of it, rather, as your natural center of being." Once you approach meditation, not with tension, but with an upward flow of self-offering, it will feel natural to rest in God's peace within.

So, remember to relax upward. Perhaps in your own hour of need, or at any unexpected moment, you'll find a blessed gift from the Divine Hand.

Your friend in God,
NAYASWAMI DEVI

GIVE GOD THE RESPONSIBILITY

D evi and I have been exploring the same basic theme for three blogs, allowing us to look more deeply at such an important topic. Two weeks ago I wrote about the importance of faith, followed by Devi's blog about relaxing upward. Today, I want to write about a topic that concerns everyone: how to deal with our responsibilities.

The teachings of the scriptures and the Masters are quite clear on the topic: We have a responsibility to act to the best of our ability, with righteousness and with kindness toward all. Of course, we have to do our best to foresee the likely results of our actions, but then we must leave the results to God. We can't control the thoughts and reactions of others.

Imagine a lighthouse: The keeper has to make sure that the light is operating well and is sending out its beam. But he isn't responsible for the actions of every ship's captain. Likewise, we need to project our light, and leave the rest to God.

Last week we received a lovely letter from a friend that illustrates the point. She is a doctor and the medical officer for a large business in southern India. I've excerpted from her letter:

> There are many young girls working here and they have a lady welfare officer. This LWO is very friendly to me and a very nice person. One day I saw her at her workplace and was shocked to see how she was interacting with her subordinate girls. She seemed totally different. She was shouting at them with no basic respect at all and also showing irritation and anger towards them in words and actions.
>
> When she later came to my cabin, I told her that I was surprised that she behaves like that with those girls. She said that's how we can get the work done from these people otherwise they cheat us. I just thought it's difficult to change people with such a strong mind-set. I was judgmental at that time.
>
> I had the book *Touch of Love* on my table, intending to read it during my free time. My friend saw the book and quickly ran through the pages. She said that she reads a lot and so I offered her the book.
>
> In a week's time she came back and she said it's such a lovely book and asked me about the path and about the authors of the book!
>
> She said it has touched her so much that she should start being good and kind, especially to her girls and not shout at them with harsh words. I was so surprised and happy as I could see that gentleness in her eyes too.

Dear Jyotish ji and Devi ji, I am so happy that you are changing lives, knowingly and unknowingly in many corners of the world, through the light of Master and Swamiji. I have been having that book for a year and she took it, read and got the essence of it in no time. I have been wanting to tell you this. It's really so joyful at heart to actually see someone changing to become better .

Thanks to You and Master and Swamiji for spreading this love and light.

God knows how to do His work in the hearts and souls of all His children. We should play our roles as well as possible, and act with pure intentions. Be like a lighthouse shining your light into the darkness. But then leave the results and the responsibility to God.

In the light,
NAYASWAMI JYOTISH

38
September 24, 2021

WHAT AM I SUPPOSED TO LEARN?

Little did I know, that first day I arrived at Ananda Village — July 4, 1969 — that my real education and, in fact, my real life was about to begin. Twenty-two years old, I had just finished college. Up until then I had basically spent my whole life listening to teachers feed me facts, figures, theories, and formulae. Though I'd excelled in my studies, I was weary of the kind of education that was imposed from the outside, never even scratching the surface of what I really wanted to know.

This was now to change very quickly. As I listened to Swami Kriyananda impart the teachings of Paramhansa Yogananda, a new understanding of life started to unfold within me. It was as though a door opened in my consciousness, and I began to realize how much there was to learn: about myself, about the nature of reality, about the true purpose of life.

It wasn't only the subjects that Swamiji addressed, but the *way* he taught them: seeking always to awaken the innate understanding within each of us. Later he explained that all true wisdom is *smriti*, or memory, and that an enlightened teacher tries to help his students remember what they already know within themselves.

116

I remember an early talk in which he posed the question: "What lessons are we supposed to learn in this great school of life?" What a wonderful question, and what wonderful answers he gave: "How to be happy in yourself"; "How to get along with others"; "How to be helpful and not harmful in the things you do and the way you treat others"; and "How to be calm when the world seems to be falling apart around you."

Swamiji went on to say, "All of these will help you to attain that state of centeredness from which you will be able to rise to your highest vibration."

So, how do we know what our particular lessons are in this lifetime? They will, of course, be different for each one of us depending on our karma. Here are some guidelines for identifying them:

1. Look at issues that come up repeatedly and that leave you unsettled or unsure of yourself. What is the common thread?

2. Find areas in yourself that tend to produce disharmony with others. In which situations are you unable to see others' realities?

3. Be aware of the times in which you feel you are compromising your integrity. In what areas of life do you allow yourself to lower your standards of behavior?

4. With honesty, bring to the light things that you try to hide from yourself, from others, and from God. Why don't you trust that God sees and accepts you exactly as you are?

After considering what you came to learn, here are some tips to help you handle your "lesson plan":

1. If a problem arises repeatedly, as soon as it begins to assert itself, get centered and take control before you get caught. Be proactive, not reactive.

2. Visualize yourself handling the situation in a calm and effective way. Marathon runners often visualize themselves crossing the finish line with a specific time goal in mind. See yourself successfully passing your life tests.

3. Commit yourself to learning your lessons and to changing. It took a long time to create the problems before you. Now put out the time and energy necessary to overcome them.

4. Examine your inner strengths to see how you can use them to support the areas where you need help. Build on your successes, and you'll gain confidence along the way. And

5. Perhaps most importantly, pray for God's grace to help you understand your karmic lessons and to give you the inner clarity to learn them well.

Don't feel overwhelmed by how much you may need to learn. We've been placed in this "great school of life" to find joy and freedom from all limitations. Know that the Divine Teacher has been silently, lovingly, unceasingly drawing out your own innate wisdom to help you pass all your tests.

Swami Kriyananda wrote: "When troubles beset you, seek both their cause and their solution in yourself. . . . Don't upset yourself with life's complexity, but seek the divine simplicity of oneness with God's joy."

At the end of the day, what are we supposed to learn? To love. To trust. To find joy in everything. Then will we be able to say with simplicity, "I have learned what I wanted to know. Now I am ready to go home."

With God's love and joy,
NAYASWAMI DEVI

39

October 1, 2021

IDENTITY THEFT

T his blog is meant to be what Master said life should be: "entertaining and educational." It is done in a light way about a serious topic, but sometimes things are too serious to be approached seriously. So, here is a story of the journey of a young man that Swami Kriyananda might have called, "devotee everyone." For the sake of brevity, we'll call him simply "Seeker." I hope you enjoy it.

At the station:

Seeker: "I want to report an identity theft."

Police officer: "We're getting a lot of reports of that these days. What did they get? Social Security number? Driver's license? Credit cards?"

Seeker: "Actually, it's more subtle than that. I'm not missing any of the stuff that can be replaced. I think someone has taken the memory of my identity, of who I really am. I think they must have used some kind of drug or hypnosis."

Officer: "Unless there's some physical evidence, we can't help. Confidentially, some of the guys here get those same thoughts from time to time. When we feel like that, we try music—good and loud, or binge-watching a T.V. series, even surfing the internet—anything to distract ourselves."

Seeker: "I don't think that's going to help me."

Officer: (Whispering as he walks him to the door) "Listen, my wife goes to this psychiatrist. Here's her card."

At the clinic:

Psychiatrist: "How may I help you?"

Seeker: (Explains the situation) "I can't quite put my finger on it, but sometimes I get a sense that I'm somebody else."

Psychiatrist: "Who?"

Seeker: (Mumbling) "A son of God."

Psychiatrist: "If you think you're the Son of God, that's what we call a 'delusion of grandeur.' It's not easy to treat."

Seeker: "Not *the* son of God. *A* son of God — a child of God."

Psychiatrist: "I've had others with this problem, but I've never had any success working with them. I can give you something for the anxiety, but it won't treat the underlying problem. My husband has the same issues and seems to get some help from a spiritual teacher. Here's his card."

At the ashram:

Spiritual teacher: "How may I help you?"

Seeker: Explains his feelings.

Spiritual teacher: "I think I can help, and have some techniques that really work, especially meditation. But it will take time, effort, and dedication. Are you willing?"

Seeker: "Yes, I'm desperate. I'll do anything."

Spiritual teacher: "To start with, I'm going to ask you to peer into this globe. Your job is to see a silver-white star in the very center. Some sages have said that this is the true Star of Bethlehem that led the three wise men to the Christ child, or Son of God."

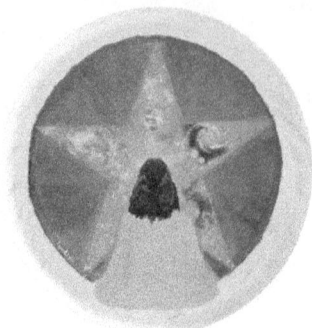

"King of the Infinite,"
by Nayaswami Jyotish.

Seeker: (After a few minutes of looking into the globe) "The surface is all clouded and disturbed. I can't see into the center at all."

Spiritual teacher: "Your first problem is that you have to sit still. It's your movement that is disturbing the light."

Seeker: "It's better now, but the light on the surface roils."

Spiritual teacher: "The light is reacting to your breath. Just observe the breath coming in and out. That will help you withdraw your life force and focus your mind."

Seeker: (Some days later) "It's getting better. I can see deeper into the globe, but now I keep seeing flashes of light that I didn't notice before."

Spiritual teacher: "The globe is reacting to your restless thoughts. You have to learn to withdraw from the sensory input in order to focus more deeply."

Seeker: (After several months) "I still have far to go, but I have some periods where I can see the star. When I'm really focused, it's almost as if I'm becoming the light. I still have a ways to go to get to that state you call 'smriti,' but at least it feels like I have a pathway forward."

In a shop a year later:

Police officer: "Hey, I remember you. Did you ever find any solution for that 'identity theft' you came in about?"

Seeker: "Well, one thing led to another and I found out what

122

was going on. I feel a little silly that I came to you. It turns out that I simply forgot who I really am, so I'm working with some memory techniques."

Officer: (Laughing) "I could probably use some of those myself, especially after a tough day or a long night."

Seeker: "Well, if you ever feel ready, let me know. In the meantime, I know this couple who write an interesting weekly blog. . . ."

In divine friendship,
NAYASWAMI JYOTISH

COLLABORATION

"You should write a book on collaborative medicine." Swami Kriyananda once gave this advice to Dr. Peter Van Houten, the physician for Ananda Village, and the founder of a national award–winning rural clinic.

Recently we had an inspiring visit with Peter and his wife, Patricia, during which he shared about how he practices medicine "collaboratively" at his clinic. First, there's the aspect of having practitioners from multiple fields — dentists, behavioral therapists, as well as doctors and nurses — who all work together as a team.

If, for example, a doctor feels that a patient's physical problems stem from mental health issues, he or she will do a "warm handoff" to a behavioral therapist. Using this method, the follow-through rate of getting treatment and overcoming health challenges is extremely high.

But there's a deeper aspect to collaborative medicine that has spiritual implications as well. Peter said that the clinic staff tries to form a bond of friendship and respect with each patient. Rather than just proclaiming as a medical expert, "You must take this medicine," or, "You must stop that habit," they involve the patient in the process, encouraging them to draw on their own understanding of themselves.

Peter said, "Because the patient feels respected and heard, they will often come up with a strategy that I also feel is the right one to take." Together they come up with solutions in which the patient feels he or she is participating and using their own initiative.

As Peter spoke, I began thinking of how this collaborative approach was an underlying theme in much of what Swami Kriyananda created.

In the "Education for Life" system he founded, the teacher tries to see each student as an individual with unique strengths and weaknesses. Rather than employing the "one size fits all" method of education, an "EFL" teacher works with each child to draw out their own interests and thoughts about how they need to grow and develop. Over decades we've seen self-confident, strong, and happy adults emerging from this system.

Exploring another area — learning how to communicate and create harmony with others — Swamiji wrote, "If you really want to communicate with others, seek also to *commune* with them. *Feel* their consciousness. Appreciate them for what they are and for what they do, not only for what they say." We might call this approach "collaborative communication," in which we don't talk *at* another person (especially when we disagree), but *listen* and remain open to their point of view. Swamiji defined maturity as the ability to tune in to other people's realities.

In creating the Sevaka (Renunciate) Order for members of Ananda communities, he listed four vows: *simplicity, self-control, service, and cooperative obedience.* "Cooperative obedience," he wrote, "means intelligent, creative participation in whatever one is asked to do, as opposed to that kind of obedience which asks, and is allowed to ask, no questions." Here we see the same concept of collaboration being expressed as a way for community members to live and serve together.

Finally, we come to our meditation practice and search for God. If we passively wait for God to appear, expecting Him/Her to tell us what to do, we may wait a long time. But if we join our energy with God's through "intelligent, creative participation," our inner life becomes a dynamic partnership with the Divine.

God, then, like the good doctor practicing "collaborative medicine" with his patients, subtly "leans in" to draw out our innate wisdom. Through respected teachers, compassionate friends, and our own wisdom-guided intuition, the Divine Physician helps us make the right choices and walk the spiritual path with strength and confidence.

Yoganandaji wrote, "Be still, and let God answer you within. Learn to know Him by the extent to which you know your true, inner Self."

May we all be healed of soul ignorance and find the Self within.

NAYASWAMI DEVI

START WITH THE HEART

It seems nearly impossible to stop the restless monkey mind during meditation. Why? In part, because we are looking at the effect rather than the cause. Mental restlessness is generally initiated by restless emotions! If you want to calm an agitated mind, first see what emotions are triggering your thoughts. Start with the heart.

I practiced this principle in my meditation this morning. Instead of trying to quell my restless mind mentally, I simply observed the feelings in my heart. I quickly saw what was provoking my train of thought. I proceeded to physically relax the heart area, and then used a very simple pranayama (regular breathing) to further calm my heart center. It worked like magic — my mind immediately quieted down and became focused. Swami Kriyananda often told us that reason follows feeling.

The great masters open the heart first, knowing that the mind will follow. There is a beautiful example of this in the book *Sometimes Brilliant*. The author, Larry Brilliant, became a disciple of the great saint Neem Karoli Baba. At first repulsed by Maharaji, as he was called, Larry had a miraculous conversion and, following his guru's instructions, went on to help eradicate smallpox in India.

His great awakening came during his first physical contact with the Master: "I began to shiver. The tingling intensity, rising up my spine like mercury in a thermometer. I could barely feel my fingers. . . . He opened his eyes wide and our gaze locked.

Light seemed to pour out of him into me and I felt like I was being filled with love upon love. . . . When he saw that I was full, he broke the contact like nothing had happened, giggled, and tugged harder on my beard. . . . I felt loved like never before, completely understood, naked and unashamed. Tears streamed down my face."

Likewise, Yogananda's first experience of cosmic consciousness began in his heart center: "Master spoke caressively, comfortingly. His calm gaze was unfathomable. 'Your heart's desire shall be fulfilled.' . . . He struck gently on my chest above the heart. My body became immovably rooted; breath was drawn out of my lungs as if by some huge magnet. Soul and mind instantly lost their physical bondage, and streamed out like a fluid piercing light from my every pore."

Learn to observe the feelings in your heart.

How can we expand our hearts, deepen our meditations, and become open to God's love? Here are some simple suggestions:

1. Learn to observe the feelings in your heart. Know that this is where restlessness starts, whether in meditation or in daily life.

2. Catch your emotional reactions quickly! As with other skills, the more you practice this, the more adept you will become.

3. First, shift your feelings into neutral, neither positive nor negative. The heart is the pivotal point from which the energy can flow in either an upward and expansive direction or a downward and contractive one. As in a car, you need to shift into neutral before you can move into forward or reverse. During my meditation, the relaxation and regular breathing shifted me into neutral, and from there I could redirect my energy upward.

4. If you want deeper meditations, change from thinking to observing: *Watch* the breath, *listen* to AUM, *feel* the Kriya currents, or *look* into the light of the spiritual eye. The spiritual states we yearn for lie behind the fringe of the mind.

5. Being able to control the reactive process imparts two huge benefits: the power to remain even-minded and cheerful, and the ability to choose to be happy in all situations.

Let us follow Swami Kriyananda's advice in his song "In the Temple of Isis": "Still your heart if you want to pray. Send all cares far away."

From the heart,
NAYASWAMI JYOTISH

HIDING IN PLAIN SIGHT

Some years ago our four-year-old son came to me with an odd expression on his face and said, "I didn't do nuffing, Mommy." His transparent attempt to appear innocent gave him away, and I asked, "*Where* didn't you do nothing?"

Looking down, he admitted, "In the closet."

We went there straightaway to discover what mischief he had gotten into. A quick glance revealed that he had taken all the bottles of vitamin pills and dumped them out into great heaps on the closet floor.

I enjoy sharing this story because in the innocence of a child's mind, we see a reflection of our own efforts to hide our mistakes. Whether silly lapses or mortal sins, we hope that no one, especially not God, sees our errors. Yet in this attempt to cover things up, we carry within us the burden of guilt, shame, and self-blame.

I'm not suggesting that we broadcast our failings to the world, but there is another way to drop the millstone of guilt that hangs around our neck. Without fear of judgment or rejection, we can offer all our past wrong actions to God. In truth, He knows about them already. And He will probably be as amused as we were with our son.

In *Paramhansa Yogananda: A Biography*, Swami Kriyananda wrote: "I can vouch for his perfect knowledge of the thoughts and actions of his disciples. He once said to me, 'I know every thought you think!' And he proved that statement again and again. Once at Hollywood Church I told an insincere member that I would be giving next Wednesday's class. 'In that case,' the member said, 'I will be sure to come.' Well, I knew he would have come anyway; therefore it irritated me slightly that he would pretend to be coming only because I would be giving the class. Wanting to deflect his insincere flattery from myself, I answered him (not very elegantly, I'm afraid), 'In that case, would you please stand outside and check people's pockets for vegetables as they come in?'

"A few days later I was with my guru while he entertained guests for lunch. After they'd left, as I sat at the table alone with him, he remarked to me casually, 'By the way, when you are talking with a congregation member, don't talk about vegetables! It isn't dignified.'"

So if God and Guru already know about our mistakes, why do we need to tell them? Because by trusting that God has only our highest welfare in mind, we begin to dissolve the protective shell that the ego has created to defend itself. By offering up to God our missteps, we no longer need to carry them as subconscious burdens. Gradually, as we let down our defenses, the ego gains a transparency and innocence that is the mark of true saints.

There's a story from the life of St. Joseph of Cupertino, a great saint, who in his simplicity was often the butt of practical jokes from his fellow monks. One day as he was doing his chores in cleaning the stables, a group of them came to tease him.

"Come quick, Joseph. There's a cow flying in the sky," the monks said, trying hard to suppress their laughter. Rushing out of the stables, Joseph looked and looked, but could see no flying cow. Finally unable to contain their laughter, one of them said, "You simpleton! Don't you know that cows can't fly?"

With the guilelessness of a child, Joseph replied, "I'd rather think that cows could fly than that my brother monks would lie to me."

Stung to the quick, the taunting monks departed, shamefaced.

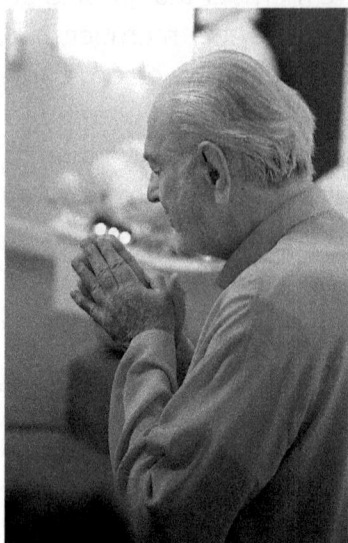

Knowing that God already sees everything that we're trying to hide, have the courage to open your heart completely to Him. Believe that Divine Mother won't punish you for any foolish actions, but will help you to make better choices in the future.

In a beautiful essay that Swami Kriyananda wrote towards the end of his life, "Why I Love My Guru, Paramhansa Yogananda," he says: "He [Yoganandaji] was ever, and is now more than ever, my nearest, dearest companion. If I am right, I feel his inner smile. If I am wrong, I feel his inner encouragement to do better.

"He is *on my side* in every struggle against delusion. Could anyone be a better, truer friend than that?"

What a great reassurance to accept that God knows us, sees us to our very depths, and still He is on our side in our efforts to overcome delusion. There's no need to try to hide anything, because we stand forever in His loving sight.

With joy,
NAYASWAMI DEVI

SHARING SHIVA

There is a beautiful Shiva shrine at Ananda Village, a sacred place where many have meditated over the years. It is larger than life size and was sculpted by a talented artist who lived here. Michael, a longtime Village resident, lives nearby, and by helping tend it has developed a deep connection with this image of God. Some years back, he also acquired a lovely little murti of his beloved Shiva that had been abandoned, and it has been a central feature of his meditation room. A year or more ago he felt the inspiration to share the blessings that come from the statue, and has asked a number of people if they would like to "caretake" Shiva for a few weeks.

When he called us recently, he said something very perceptive. "I noticed that in the last several days, I haven't thought about Shiva. I think my lack of attention means that he wants to move to a new home for a while. Would you like to take him?" And so Shiva now sits in our meditation room, radiating his blessings to us. I always try to bow to him, along with our other masters, before I leave the silence and start the day's business.

As you know, Devi and I alternate the week when we write the blog. There is a little secret that we should keep quiet, so please don't spread it around: Unfortunately, we often don't know what to write about and sometimes struggle to find an inspiring theme. I was in the midst of this dilemma, but this morning as I was bowing to Shiva preparing to leave the meditation room, he whispered the thought, "Why don't you write about me, and about sharing inspiration?"

Sharing our inspiration with others is central to our spiritual growth. It is a spiritual law that the things we share grow stronger, and those that we hoard to ourselves shrivel up and die. When we share that which inspires us it not only grows stronger within us, but multiplies its power. Thanks to Michael, there are now many residents who have been blessed by his murti.

The inspiration we share rarely has a physical form. Usually it is an encounter, a story, a technique, or a new insight. Where would we all be if Paramhansa Yogananda had not shared his wisdom and insights with Swami Kriyananda or with us? The selfless sharing of love from a mother and father makes it possible for life to survive. But there is also the opposite tendency, to be greedy with the gifts we have been given.

Each week our Sunday service ends with a reading of the Festival of Light, written by Swami Kriyananda. In this ceremony there is a passage that depicts the journey of the soul. Swamiji has written it in poetic form as the story of a little bird. For the bird, as for every soul, there comes a time, before wisdom has had a chance to grow, when it rebels. "What else is wisdom," it decides, "if not to keep what is mine for myself?"

So, friends, every day we have a choice to make. Should we rebel and keep what is ours for ourselves, or should we share Shiva? If you look at the smile on Shiva's photo, you will see his answer.

In the joy of sharing,
NAYASWAMI JYOTISH

THE PRINCIPLE OF T.W.O.

It was July 31, 1949. Paramhansa Yogananda had been invited to speak at, of all places, a Beverly Hills society garden party. His hostess expected him, no doubt, to make a few gracious remarks to her guests, who could then get on with their socializing. Were they in for a surprise!

Swami Kriyananda writes about this event in *The New Path*:

> Never had I imagined that the power of human speech could be so overwhelming; it was the most moving talk I have ever heard.
>
> "This day," he [Yoganandaji] thundered, punctuating every word, "marks the birth of a new era. My spoken words are registered in the ether, in the Spirit of God, and they shall move the West. . . . We must go on — not only those who are here, but thousands of youths must go North, South, East, and West to cover the earth with little colonies, demonstrating that simplicity of living plus high thinking lead to the greatest happiness!"
>
> I was stirred to my very core. . . . Deeply I vowed that day to do my utmost to make his words a reality.

Thus began Swami Kriyananda's determined effort to create such communities. This ultimately led to the founding of Ananda Village on July 4, 1969 — almost exactly twenty years after that garden party speech.

Actually, Swamiji had been interested in starting communities from his youth, but it was more of an ideal than an active pursuit. It wasn't until the power of Master's *thoughts* charged him with the *willpower and energy* to build "colonies" that he dedicated his life to this mission.

For the next forty years, he strove to manifest Master's vision and founded what are now flourishing communities in America, Europe, and India. With a tireless flow of energy and willpower, he overcame every obstacle that confronted him with determination and courage.

But there was another aspect to his ability to make this dream a reality: *self-offering*. Everything he undertook was done in service to Yoganandaji, and with the consciousness that God, not he, was the Doer. In this way he drew on a constant flow of guidance, creativity, and grace to accomplish his goals in serving his guru.

This brings us to the Principle of T.W.O., which stands for using the power of *Thought + Will + Offering* to succeed in realizing our goals.

Here's how you can apply this principle in your own life.

First, *think* about something you'd like to accomplish that feels in tune with higher principles. Visualize your goal clearly at the spiritual eye. If the overall project seems too big for you, break it down into small, doable steps that you can take to reach your goal.

Next, summon up the *willingness and energy* needed to move forward step by step. If you encounter problems or obstacles, don't get discouraged. Instead, expect challenges to come along. Then, when they do, go deeper within to find hidden reservoirs of strength and determination to break through whatever barriers threaten to stop your progress. Master said that every test we face is a test of our willpower. Match whatever adverse circumstances life throws at you with enough energy to emerge victorious.

Finally, *offer* to God your thoughts and energy for His guidance and blessing. Everything we do is really only a part of His dream. Once when an Ananda community leader was being faced with some challenges, Swamiji said to her, "Remember, this work isn't your work. It isn't my work. It is the work of Babaji and Master." If we can remember that God is the Doer, we will feel an underlying wave of support that brings us to the shores of fulfillment.

What is the ultimate benefit of using the T.W.O. formula? Beyond any outward success, we will find a deepening sense of attunement and unity with divine consciousness. Thus, T.W.O. is transformed into greater awareness of being ONE with God.

In divine friendship,
NAYASWAMI DEVI

KARMIC SEEDS

D evi and I were giving a series of programs at our community and temple in Palo Alto, California, a few days ago. As all the events of the weekend were winding down something very touching took place. In a conspiratorial and somewhat excited manner, they led us to two chairs set in front of a small choir in their courtyard.

When they began to sing it brought tears to my eyes. About a year ago I had rewritten the lyrics to a traditional song called "Shenandoah," which has a lovely, haunting melody — the new words reflecting a longing for Divine Mother rather than the traditional love of a man for a woman. After the words had come to me, I shared them in a blog called "Seeing Spirit Everywhere." Here they are:

> O Divine Mother, I long to know You.
> Fade away, O world of maya.
> Divine Mother, I long to know You.
> Away, I'm bound away into the deep sushumna.
>
> O Divine Mother, I long to see You.
> Fade away, O gaudy maya.
> Divine Mother, I long to see You.
> Away, I'm bound away through the bright Kutastha.
>
> O Divine Mother, I long to hear You.
> Fade away, O noise of maya.

Divine Mother, I long to hear You.
Away, I'm bound away to merge into the bliss of AUM.

What made the experience in Palo Alto particularly special for me was the completely unexpected return of an old friend. For Devi and me these blogs are a little like our spiritual children. Once they "leave home" we don't really expect to see them again. We release our blogs into the ether without any attachment, although we deeply appreciate the comments people might make about a particular post.

"*Master in the Springtime,*"
by *Nayaswami Jyotish.*

Isn't it true, friends, that many things in life seem very ephemeral? An event, or a creative idea comes, has its little moment on the stage of our life's experiences, and then passes into memory where it dims and fades away. Although I had rewritten the words to this song, I had never heard it performed. And I never expected to.

But the great masters teach us that our every thought, word, or deed plants a karmic seed. In one way or another, these seeds are destined to return to us. We are usually more aware of the negative seeds than of the positive ones. Our past errors seem to come back to us like a winter storm, full of sound and fury. But most of the time our positive karma seems to slip in unnoticed.

Every once in a while, however, a kernel of positive karma from the past makes a special visit home. Perhaps, as in this case, a group of friends go to considerable effort to give us a lovely surprise. They sit us down, have us pay attention, and then give us a gift of love like this song. An event like this helps to wake us up.

God is always waiting for us, wanting to help us be happy. Long ago, I had written words of longing to Divine Mother, and here She was in the form of these friends singing them back to me. If we pay attention, we will see that Divine Mother visits us every day. Let us try to listen for Her footsteps and hear Her song.

In appreciation,
NAYASWAMI JYOTISH

P.S. Here is a link to a recording of the song: **crystalclarity.com/133**.

THE NIGHTINGALE

T his past week has been a time of introspection for us. Nayaswami Seva, our dear friend of more than fifty years and one of Ananda's founding members, passed away suddenly last Sunday of a heart attack. Though eighty-six years old, she was in good health and was still serving dynamically throughout the community.

The example of her life and her determination to find God will be a guiding light for all of us.

Shortly after arriving at Ananda in 1970, Seva became a renunciate and followed that path for the rest of her days. Ever-joyful, ever-giving, ever-loving, Seva was a beautiful role model for living for God alone. As one friend put it, "She was a saint who walked among us." Though she will be deeply missed, the example of her life and her determination to find God will be guiding lights for all of us.

Today I went to the Crystal Hermitage gardens to contemplate Seva's passing. Hers was not an easy life, for she had many tests, but she triumphed spiritually over them all.

As I sat on a small bench gazing out at the beautiful fall colors and the calm, clear sky, the radiant red leaves of a Japanese maple tree fell silently around me. Tears began to fall silently from my eyes as well, but they were not tears of sorrow at her loss. Rather they were tears of gratitude for the gifts of divine friendship, of life, and of seeking the reality beyond life and death. As this gratitude filled my heart, I began to think of other episodes in my life that had at first seemed to be filled with loss, but turned out to be great gifts.

When the forest fire struck Ananda Village in 1976, most of us lost everything we had. Trying to move past a sense of loss, I realized that any security based on material possessions is forever unreliable. With God's grace, I understood that a sense of security within is the only bedrock on which we can rely. This gift has remained with me ever since.

Over the years when there have been misunderstandings or disharmony with family members or friends, those experiences, too, have been transformed. Invariably as time passed, I discovered the gift of unconditional love for those involved, and a deeper soul bond grew as we worked together through past karma.

I could name many more such episodes from my life, but with Thanksgiving approaching, I invite you to give thanks for things in your own life for which you're grateful. Think especially about those experiences that seemed difficult at first, but turned out to be blessings.

A friend of mine at Ananda Village, Erin, told me that she has a daily practice of writing in a journal that she calls her "Little Book of Gratitude." Every day she writes down at least three things for which she's grateful, some of which are challenges. She said that over time this practice has filled her with joy as she's come to realize how filled with gifts life really is. Perhaps you'd like to start your own "Little Book of Gratitude" to see what you can learn from it.

Swami Kriyananda wrote a beautiful song called "The Song of the Nightingale." In the introduction he said, "If you would hear the nightingale thrilling the air with liquid melodies, be not afraid to listen to the night." Here are the lyrics to the first two stanzas:

Nightingale! Nightingale!
    Sing of joy through the night.
Teach my heart
To impart
    Ev'rywhere your delight.
Sing of moonrays on the rain.
Sing that love's not in vain.
Ev'ry grief, ev'ry wrong
Has its ending in song.

Nightingale! Nightingale!
    Sing of joy through the night.
Teach all men
How to spin
    Clouds of gloom into light.
Without silence, what is song?
Without night, where is dawn?
Were it not for men's woes,
Who would smile at a rose?

Nayaswami Seva was like that nightingale who learned to sing with joy in spite of every test that she faced. So, my friends, let's remember to look for God's hidden blessings behind "every grief" and "every wrong." Let's join "our nightingale" in singing a song of gratitude for each experience that comes so that we, too, can triumph and find freedom in God.

Wishing you a blessed time of Thanksgiving,
NAYASWAMI DEVI

DIVERSITY AND UNITY

There is a yearning in our hearts for a better world than the one we see around us. This longing burns especially brightly when daily headlines are filled with such negativity, division, and anger. When I was in college I wrote an essay about a Utopian world where suddenly everyone was able to communicate telepathically. After a period of turbulence, this brought about world understanding and peace. Little did I know at the time that the consciousness of the great masters already lives in such a world.

In 1926, Yogananda gave a talk in Cincinnati, Ohio, entitled, "How to Live Several Hundred Years in Advance of Your Times." People flocked to hear him, surely looking forward with "hope for a better world," to quote the title of one of Swami Kriyananda's books.

At Ananda Village we are actively confronting the polarization, prejudice, and hatred of our times and have formed an *Ananda Diversity and Inclusion Council*. We recently held our first meeting with representatives from various subgroups that live here: African American, Asian, LGBT+, Indian, and even someone representing the elders. People are not their skin color, tendencies, age, or national origin, but in today's world it is important to affirm our unity.

During our meeting, one of the most thrilling moments came when the organizer, Nefretete, read a letter from a student in India who is part of Ananda's international high school. I thought you would like to see what she wrote:

What Diversity Means to Me

Whether we all descend from different cultures, have different heritages, or live in different countries, we all have one common thread that ignores the boundaries of physical demographics and nationalities. The one common thread that brings us all together and unites our diverse backgrounds is the ideology of Self-Realization. Self-Realization is a path of spiritual renewal and recognition of the highest levels of Oneself. The spiritual path does not specify any gender, race, or religion that is exclusively entitled to experiencing Self-Realization. The diverse values and inclusion of many cultural communities is a multivocal process that we can all choose to experience. Swamiji spoke about his vision of creating world brotherhood communities and colonies that support high thinking and simple living. I believe that a part of Self-Realization is recognizing that we all are unique, yet similar in our ways of thinking and acting. We may not come from the same place but we all aim to reach the same place—the place of ultimate truth and wisdom—to be One in God's Light someday. Ananda has established the Diversity and Inclusion Council to encourage and support these Aims. —Manmohini Tiwari, age: 15, friend of ADIC

Isn't it wonderful to hear such wisdom from a teenager? One solution to today's problems is to train and empower a new generation filled with people like Manmohini shining the light of higher consciousness.

Let us always see the unity that hides behind His glittering diversity.

Helping create a unified world was one of Yogananda's central goals and he did everything in his power to bring it about. When Devi and I received the Global Ambassador Peace Award at the United Nations, we read Yogananda's "Prayer for a United World." Here is an excerpt:

> May the heads of all countries and races be guided to understand that men of all nations are physically and spiritually one: physically one, because we are the descendants of common parents — the symbolic Adam and Eve; spiritually one because we are the immortal children of our Father; bound by eternal links of brotherhood . . .

> In our hearts we can all learn to be free from hate and selfishness. Let us pray for harmony among the nations that they march hand in hand through the gate of a fair new civilization.

Yesterday was Thanksgiving. Let us give thanks for God's wonders of creation. And let us always see the unity that hides behind His glittering diversity.

In Divine Love,
NAYASWAMI JYOTISH

A WORLD WITHOUT
AUTOBIOGRAPHY OF A YOGI

We did an interview recently with our good friend, Phil Goldberg, author of *The Life of Yogananda: The Story of the Yogi Who Became the First Modern Guru*. The interview was in honor of the seventy-fifth anniversary of the first publication of *Autobiography of a Yogi* in December 1946.

During the interview Phil raised an interesting question: "What would the world be like today without the *Autobiography*?" This intriguing query launched a series of thoughts that kept falling like dominos in my mind for many days.

First, there are the big, bold strokes of famous people inspired by the book who have had a huge impact on society.

Steve Jobs, the visionary behind Apple, read the *Autobiography* every year of his adult life. It was the only book he kept on his iPhone, and he left instructions to give a copy of it to everyone who attended his funeral when he died tragically at an early age.

Gene Roddenberry, the creator of *Star Trek*, once gave an interview to a young actor (who happened to be a disciple of Yoganandaji). The actor saw a copy of the *Autobiography* on a bookshelf behind Mr. Roddenberry's desk, and asked him, "Have you read that book?" He replied, "Read it? I get lots of my ideas from it. The thought of 'beaming people up' came from the chapter, 'The Resurrection of Sri Yukteswar.'"

George Harrison of the Beatles became a disciple, and the music written later in his life was influenced by this association.

Virat Kohli, the captain of India's undefeated cricket team, said of the *Autobiography*: "I love this book. A must-read for all those who are brave enough to let their thoughts and ideologies be challenged. The understanding and implementation of the knowledge in this book will change your whole perspective and life."

Yogoda students at one of Yogananda's classes in Minneapolis, October 1927. The students are bowing in "pronam," the Hindu form of greeting.

Then there are the four million copies in over thirty languages that have been sold to date. In the years that Jyotish and I have been sharing Yogananda's teachings around the world, we've met countless people everywhere who have read it.

Some have said, "Oh, I read the *Autobiography* years ago. I wish I had followed him." Others told us, "When I read it, my whole perspective on life changed." And still others quietly said, "After reading it, I have followed him as a disciple ever since." Not one person we met who had read it was untouched by its spiritual influence.

Towards the end of our interview, Phil asked us another question: What was the impact on us of our first reading of the book? Strange to say, I had never really thought deeply about this. My spontaneous reply was, "I felt like I had met my dearest friend, who combined depth, wisdom, and truth with warmth, childlike joy, and humor."

So, I offer you, too, this question to ask yourself: What impact has the *Autobiography* had on your life? Perhaps in answering it, you'll receive increased clarity and commitment in your own spiritual search.

The waves of inspiration, hope, and meaning that *Autobiography of a Yogi* has radiated out to the world since its publication have been forces of upliftment for society, whether people were aware of it or not. Its message is one of unity of all races, religions, and beliefs; of the potential of every sincere seeker to find God; and of the loving presence of Divine Consciousness behind all the seemingly dark dreams of this world.

Through his autobiography, Yogananda has created a bridge to the future where people can experience their unity with God and with one another. As he wrote in the concluding sentence of his book: "'Lord,' I thought gratefully, 'Thou hast given this monk a large family!'"

We bow at your feet, dear Master, for your gift to the world of *Autobiography of a Yogi*.

NAYASWAMI DEVI

UNCONDITIONAL LOVE

We recently honored, with a celebratory satsang, the 75th anniversary of the publication of Paramhansa Yogananda's *Autobiography of a Yogi*. I was asked to speak about one of my favorite chapters in that amazing book, "An Experience in Cosmic Consciousness."

For me, as for so many others I have met, the *Autobiography* changed my life. I had been searching my entire life for meaning, and for an understanding of the possibilities of awareness. My college studies in psychology didn't answer my questions, nor did science in general, nor, for me at least, did religion. I despaired of finding answers until someone suggested I read Yogananda's great work. It is no exaggeration to say that reading the book, and that chapter in particular, not only changed my life but shaped my entire future.

As I was preparing for my talk, I did something most of us rarely do: I not only read that chapter but studied it, thought about it, and meditated on it. I was amazed at the insights that flowed and the depth of teaching that is contained there. Those few pages really summarize the whole of spiritual evolution.

One of the most important points was how life-changing it was for Yogananda to feel his guru's unconditional love.

The chapter begins with Yogananda returning shamefacedly after having left the ashram to search for God in the Himalayas. Sri Yukteswar accepted him back, not with rebuke, but with the unconditional love of the guru for his beloved disciple. "A blissful wave engulfed me," Yogananda wrote. "I was conscious that the Lord, in the form of my guru, was expanding the small ardors of my heart into the incompressible reaches of cosmic love."

That expanded heart prepared him for the experience of cosmic consciousness that would come a few days later. As I read the chapter a new understanding came to me of the steps needed to experience samadhi.

First, there must be a deep, lifelong yearning for union with God. Even as a young boy, Yogananda sought out saints and spiritual experiences.

Next, there must be the intense practice of meditation and other spiritual techniques. As Yogananda has explained, this prepares our nervous system for the tremendous flow of energy that comes with Self-realization. If we aren't prepared, that power would burn our nerves and brain.

Then, most importantly, our hearts need to expand to hold at least a tiny cup of the infinite vastness of Divine Love.

It is amusing and confusing to see how the actual experience came to Mukunda (Yogananda's boyhood name). One assumes that such a state comes as the culmination of a long, ever-deepening meditation, as it did for the Buddha. But not for Yogananda:

> A few mornings later I made my way to Master's empty sitting room. I planned to meditate, but my laudable purpose was unshared by disobedient thoughts. They scattered like birds before the hunter.

"Mukunda!" Sri Yukteswar's voice sounded from a distant inner balcony.

I felt as rebellious as my thoughts. "Master always urges me to meditate," I muttered to myself. "He should not disturb me when he knows why I came to his room." He summoned me again; I remained obstinately silent. The third time his tone held rebuke.

"I know how you are meditating," my guru called out, "with your mind distributed like leaves in a storm! Come here to me."

[Yogananda made his way, again shamefacedly, to his guru.] "Poor boy, the mountains couldn't give what you wanted. . . . Your heart's desire shall be fulfilled." . . .

He struck gently on my chest above the heart.

And then there followed the experience in cosmic consciousness that fulfilled his life's longing, changed mine, and started a worldwide spiritual revolution.

This chapter is very comforting. Like Yogananda returning shamefacedly to his guru, many struggle with the feeling that they have disappointed God—that our meditations are not deep enough, or that we have not done adequate service. But the Lord, as Sri Yukteswar demonstrated, has nothing but unconditional love for us. When we can accept that, the small ardors of our heart will begin to expand into the incompressible reaches of cosmic love.

With love and joy,
NAYASWAMI JYOTISH

P.S. You can watch my longer talk on this chapter at
crystalclarity.com/134.

WHERE TWO OR MORE
ARE GATHERED TOGETHER

Ah, Christmas: the season of social gatherings, gift giving, wonderful food, glittering decorations, hustle and bustle . . . and yet it is so much more than any of these things.

Paramhansa Yogananda said that at this time of year the Christ consciousness is especially close to earth, and more accessible to those who reach for it. And he gave a mystical explanation of Christ's statement, "Where two or three are gathered together in my name, there *am* I in the midst of them." Christ wasn't referring merely to his physical presence here. The deeper meaning is that when two or more *of our thoughts* are gathered together to focus on Christ, we will experience his presence within us.

So during this time of heightened spiritual opportunity, how do we focus more fully on him? First, we can try to follow Jesus' example of unconditional love and forgiveness. In a beautiful prayer-poem, Yoganandaji wrote of Christ: "O Thou Great Lover of all error-torn brothers, an unseen monument of the mightiest miracle of love was established in every heart when the magic of Thy voice uttered: 'Forgive them, for they know not what they do.'"

Now is the time to forgive all those who have ever hurt or offended you. Realize that when people hurt others, no matter how grievous their offense, it is done out of ignorance. Find forgiveness and compassion for them, and pray that God show them the way out of their darkness.

Next, try to transcend any sense of division and separation from others. Though their race, religion, or beliefs may be different from your own, remember that the one spirit of God animates us all. In the prayer-poem quoted earlier, Yoganandaji went on to write: "Teach us to conquer the Satan of dividing selfishness, which prevents the gathering of all our brother-souls into the one fold of Spirit. Calling to one another by the watchword: 'Love him who loves you, and love all who love you not,' let us rally beneath the canopy of the universal oneness of the Christ."

Then, live with deep faith in God's constant love and protection. In today's uncertain times it's all too easy to grow anxious about what the future may hold. Banish any such thoughts by recalling to mind and heart Christ's immortal words in the Sermon on the Mount: "Therefore take no thought, saying, What shall we eat? or, What shall we drink? or, How shall we be clothed? . . . For your heavenly Father knoweth that ye have need of all these things. But seek ye first the kingdom of God, and his righteousness; and all these things shall be added unto you."

Swami Kriyananda once told us, "Faith is the greatest thing Jesus wanted us to learn: not blind faith in mere words, but faith born of the experience of his inner presence."

Finally, try to make Christ a living reality in your life by expressing him in your thoughts, words, and actions. Your consciousness, then, will expand to embrace his presence in each moment. Yoganandaji wrote: "Do whatever you do with the thought and peace of Christ. This Christmas behold Christ born anew in the beauty of all Nature, in your awakened wisdom, in everything which wears true beauty, and in everybody who saturates himself with the fragrance of Christ-qualities."

If you strive to gather your thoughts together in these ways, you may share with Christ's disciples their experience when he appeared in their midst after the Crucifixion, and said, "Peace be unto you."

May you have a blessed Christmas season.

With joy in God, Christ, and Guru,
NAYASWAMI DEVI

THREE VISITORS

The tiny newborn had been crying for so long that Mary feared he was ill. Yet when she placed her hand on his forehead, she felt no fever. A comforting thought flashed into her mind: "He is just frustrated: He has much to say and share, but his little tongue won't yet obey his commands." So, despite his continued crying, she laid him back in his cradle. After a few minutes his wails changed suddenly to joyful coos and gurgles.

A few moments later there came a knock on the door. Expecting yet another shepherd, Joseph sighed and rose to see who had come. He was amazed to see three dark-skinned strangers, their robes dusty from long travels.

"We have come from afar to honor the child," one of them said. In spite of their dust-covered attire, they seemed somehow not of this world, almost as if they were above it. Mary called out, "The child is lifting his little arms toward them expectantly. Let them come to him."

The child smiled and cooed as they passed him from one to the next, treating him as tenderly as if they were his parents. After a time, parents and visitors all sat together talking and laughing quietly. It seemed like they had known each other always.

There was an atmosphere of joy even though the talk soon grew serious. One of the three, the youngest and somehow also the oldest, began to talk of the future as if he saw it more clearly than the walls of the shabby stable.

"Beware of King Herod, for he is terrified of your child and will seek to kill him. You will have to flee in a few weeks. I will send you a warning in a dream."

Another said to Mary, "You must become a healer and learn to help those who are in distress. Here are some precious herbs to aid you in your work. In the future you will suffer deeply. Don't despair, for through this you will earn the compassion needed to be a source of comfort and strength to the countless people who will turn to you in their hour of need."

The third pulled a small purse from his robes, the coins clinking as he set it upon the table. "You will find this useful in the months and years ahead," he remarked with a sparkle in his eyes.

To the father their leader said, "Your son will be a great teacher and a healer of men's hearts. When he is just growing out of boyhood he will insist on going to India to visit us and learn. Your natural tendency will be to hold him back, to think he is too young for such a journey, but you must give him your blessings when that time comes."

Suddenly a large, lustrous pearl appeared in his hand. "On the day of his leaving, give him this and repeat these words: 'This is a symbol of "the pearl of great price." You must return it to the three who visited you at your birth.' He will understand the message."

From time to time, the child awoke and smiled contentedly as they cuddled him and sat him on their laps. His bright little eyes followed the conversation as if he understood everything that was being said and more.

When evening fell, the visitors said their goodbyes to the family, blessing each one in turn. The parents wept as they left: Their time together had been so short, and now it felt as if their dearest friends were departing. As the three men walked slowly down the lane, though they held no lantern, Joseph and Mary saw a golden light surrounding them and lighting the path ahead. When they closed the rickety door, they saw the same aura enveloping their tiny babe.

Joseph asked Mary, "Did you understand what they meant when they said our son would live forever and bless all nations?"

She nodded with a motherly wisdom, for the heart often understands what the mind cannot grasp. "Yes. A vision flashed into my mind of a group of people some two thousand years from now sitting together, talking and laughing just as we have this afternoon. Strange though it seems, they were celebrating our son's birthday."

Happy Christmas.

NAYASWAMI JYOTISH

MY SOUL IS MARCHING ON

n many of his past lives Paramhansa Yogananda had been a great warrior and spiritual leader of humanity. He told his disciples that he had been William the Conqueror, who stormed the beach at Hastings, England, in 1066 to establish one of the oldest continuous governments in history.

In another former life, he indicated, he was King Ferdinand III of Spain, who unified the country and drove out the invading Moors, who were a threat to Spain's Christian roots. Known for his deep piety and faith in God, Ferdinand was canonized by the Catholic Church in 1671.

Yoganandaji also said he had been the great warrior-prince Arjuna, whose battle against an evil leader and his vast armies is recounted in the Bhagavad Gita. This great scripture is an allegory of the soul's battle against, and ultimate victory over, the darkening pull of materialism that has usurped the kingdom of our consciousness. In Master's explanation of the Gita he says that Arjuna is "devotee everyman," and his battle is one that each of us must fight to achieve soul freedom.

In his incarnation in the twentieth century as Paramhansa Yogananda, Master was once again a courageous warrior—this time confronting the forces of spiritual indifference and materialism rampant in the West. Arriving on the shores of America in 1920, he soon began his "spiritual campaigns," traveling tirelessly back and forth across the country lecturing, healing,

and transforming untold thousands with the shining power of his soul's magnetism.

One of my favorite poems of Master's is called "My Soul Is Marching On." In the introduction he writes, "Never be discouraged by this motion picture of life. Salvation is for all. Just remember that no matter what happens to you, still your soul is marching on. No matter where you go, your wandering footsteps will lead you back to God. There is no other way to go."

As this year, with all of its difficulties, draws to a close, and we face the uncertain prospects of 2022, take heart by following in the footsteps of our great warrior-guru. Draw from his courage, strength, and deep faith and surrender to God.

Here are some ways to face whatever may lie ahead:

Are you worried and anxious about the future? Overcome the assaults of worry with calmness. Visualize yourself fighting by Yogananda's side, infused with his strength and courage—and with the certainty that nothing and no one can defeat you. Create your own affirmation to use when "worries howl at you."

Do you find yourself judging or condemning others whose opinions differ from your own? See yourself standing by Master's side as he reaches out to help each person as his very own. See no one as a stranger, but each and every one as your brother or sister. Treat them with acceptance and respect.

Are you troubled by political conditions and trends in the world? Look into Master's eyes and see the knowledge that God — not man — is ultimately in charge, and that His Divine Plan rooted in love will prevail in the end. Carry this understanding in your heart always.

I'll close with the last verses of Master's powerful poem:

> The flowers bloomed, then hid in gloom,
> The bounty of the trees did cease;
> Colossal men have come and gone,
> But still my soul is marching on!
>
> The aeons one by one are flying,
> My arrows one by one are gone;
> Dimly, slowly, life is fading,
> But still my soul is marching on!
>
> Darkness, death, and failures vied;
> To block my path they fiercely tried.
> My fight with jealous Nature's strong,
> But still my soul is marching on!

Your comrade-in-arms in the forces of light,
NAYASWAMI DEVI

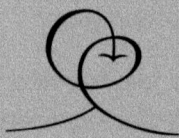

ABOUT *the* AUTHORS

Nayaswami Jyotish and Nayaswami Devi are disciples of the great master Paramhansa Yogananda (author of *Autobiography of a Yogi*) and students of Swami Kriyananda. Their mission is to help others live the teachings of Self-realization through meditation, devotion, and service.

Their lifelong dedication to the spiritual path has led them to lecture, teach, counsel, and serve throughout the world, spreading the message of peace through meditation.

They are recipients of the Global Ambassador Peace Award. This honor was conferred at the United Nations in a special ceremony by the Institute of International Social Development in recognition of their contribution to fostering world peace.

Since 1984 they have been the Spiritual Directors of Ananda Worldwide, pioneering Ananda's work in Italy and India and guiding the spiritual welfare of thousands of Yogananda's devotees. They are the co-authors of *Touch of Light, Touch of Joy, Touch of Love*, and *Touch of Peace*. To see their schedule of appearances, lectures, classes, and events online and in person, go to **jyotishanddevi.org**.

Nayaswami Jyotish was named by Swami Kriyananda as his spiritual successor after decades of helping him build Ananda's work around the world. Jyotish began taking classes from Kriyananda in 1967. In 1969 they moved together to the foothills of the Sierra Nevada Mountains of California to found Ananda Village, now a model spiritual community. Jyotish has also written several other books: *Lessons in Meditation, How to Meditate, 30-Day Essentials for Marriage,* and *30-Day Essentials for Career.*

Nayaswami Devi first met Swami Kriyananda in 1969 and dedicated her life to the spiritual path. She and Jyotish were married in 1975 and have spent their life together serving Swami Kriyananda and their guru, Paramhansa Yogananda. Devi is the author of *Faith Is My Armor: The Life of Swami Kriyananda,* and the editor of two of Swami Kriyananda's books: *Intuition for Starters* and *The Light of Superconsciousness.*

jyotishanddevi.org

FURTHER EXPLORATIONS
WITH CRYSTAL CLARITY

CRYSTAL CLARITY PUBLISHERS

If you enjoyed this title, Crystal Clarity Publishers invites you to deepen your spiritual life through many additional resources based on the teachings of Paramhansa Yogananda. We offer books, e-books, audiobooks, yoga and meditation videos, and a wide variety of inspirational and relaxation music composed by Swami Kriyananda.

See a listing of books below, visit our secure website for a complete online catalog, or place an order for our products.

crystalclarity.com
800.424.1055 | **clarity@crystalclarity.com**
1123 Goodrich Blvd. | Commerce, CA 90022

ANANDA WORLDWIDE

Crystal Clarity Publishers is the publishing house of Ananda, a worldwide spiritual movement founded by Swami Kriyananda, a direct disciple of Paramhansa Yogananda. Ananda offers resources and support for your spiritual journey through meditation instruction, webinars, online virtual community, email, and chat.

Ananda has more than 150 centers and meditation groups in over 45 countries, offering group guided meditations, classes and teacher training in meditation and yoga, and many other resources.

In addition, Ananda has developed eight residential communities in the US, Europe, and India. Spiritual communities are places where people live together in a spirit of cooperation and friendship, dedicated to a common goal. Spirituality is practiced in all areas of daily life: at school, at work, or in the home. Many Ananda communities offer internships during which one can stay and experience spiritual community firsthand.

For more information about Ananda communities or meditation groups near you, please visit **ananda.org** or call 530.478.7560.

THE EXPANDING LIGHT RETREAT

The Expanding Light is the largest retreat center in the world to share exclusively the teachings of Paramhansa Yogananda. Situated in the Ananda Village community near Nevada City, California, the center offers the opportunity to experience spiritual life in a contemporary ashram setting. The varied, year-round schedule of classes and programs on yoga, meditation, and spiritual practice includes Karma Yoga, personal retreat, spiritual travel, and online learning. Large groups are welcome.

The Ananda School of Yoga & Meditation offers certified yoga, yoga therapist, spiritual counselor, and meditation teacher trainings.

The teaching staff has years of experience practicing Kriya Yoga meditation and all aspects of Paramhansa Yogananda's teachings. You may come for a relaxed personal renewal, participating in ongoing activities as much or as little as you wish. The serene mountain setting, supportive staff, and delicious vegetarian meals provide an ideal environment for a truly meaningful stay, be it a brief respite or an extended spiritual vacation.

For more information, please visit **expandinglight.org** or call 800.346.5350.

ANANDA MEDITATION RETREAT

Set amidst seventy-two acres of beautiful meditation gardens and wild forest in Northern California's Sierra foothills, the Ananda Meditation Retreat is an ideal setting for a rejuvenating, inner experience.

The Meditation Retreat has been a place of deep meditation and sincere devotion for over fifty years. Long before that, the Native American Maidu tribe held this to be sacred land. The beauty and presence of the Divine are tangibly felt by all who visit here.

Studies show that being in nature and using techniques such as forest bathing can significantly reduce stress and blood pressure while strengthening your immune system, concentration, and level of happiness. The Meditation Retreat is the perfect place for quiet immersion in nature.

Plan a personal retreat, enjoy one of the guided retreats, or choose from a variety of programs led by the caring and joyful staff.

For more information or to place your reservation, please visit **meditationretreat.org**, email **meditationretreat@ananda.org**, or call 530.478.7557.

More Books by

Nayaswami Jyotish and Nayaswami Devi

Touch of Light

Living the Teachings of Paramhansa Yogananda
Nayaswami Jyotish and Nayaswami Devi

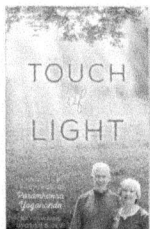

Touch of Light is taken from the popular blog entries of the same title. Like the facets of a beautiful diamond, each chapter's topic is a small reflection of the brilliance of one of the great spiritual figures of our time. Paramhansa Yogananda came to the West in 1920, bringing a new vision of how to live. He lectured across the United States drawing thousands, and filling the largest auditoriums. Even after Yogananda's passing in 1952, his *Autobiography of a Yogi* continues to inspire influential people such as George Harrison, Gene Roddenberry (creator of Star Trek), and Steve Jobs.

The authors were fortunate to have Kriyananda's training and friendship. They were also founding members of many of these communities. They know from experience that these teachings can improve all aspects of life—health, business, success, creativity, marriage, family, education, and spiritual development.

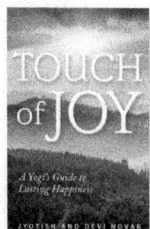

Touch of Joy

A Yogi's Guide to Lasting Happiness
Jyotish and Devi Novak

Joy is an aspect of God, and is at the heart of our own soul nature. It is not to be found in outer fulfillments or gratifications, but exists without any cause. Swami Kriyananda, a direct disciple of Yogananda and spiritual teacher of the authors, once said, "Joy is the solution, not the reward." To learn to live with joy under all circumstances, and not to wait only until conditions are to our liking, is the secret of a happy life.

The authors are celebrated lecturers who have inspired many thousands around the world. They know from experience that these teachings can improve all aspects of life—health, business, success, creativity, marriage, family, education, and spiritual development. The authors, having studied for nearly fifty years with Swami Kriyananda, are Spiritual Directors of Ananda Worldwide and live in Nevada City, California.

Touch of Love
Living the Teachings of Paramhansa Yogananda
Nayaswami Jyotish and Nayaswami Devi

We, and the very fabric of the atoms, are made from love and joy, and our hearts will never rest until we are reunited with that reality," said author Nayaswami Jyotish. When we welcome the presence of love into our lives, our entire existence is born anew.

Once again, the authors accompany us on the journey of the heart: answering the call of true, unconditional love. This book is a compilation of weekly letters they posted in 2017 and 2018 to their popular blog, A Touch of Light. The letters are filled with spiritual teachings as practical as they are profound, faithfully shared in the spirit of their beloved guru, Paramhansa Yogananda, and his direct disciple, Swami Kriyananda.

Touch of Peace
Living the Teachings of Paramhansa Yogananda
Nayaswami Jyotish and Nayaswami Devi

Tales of forgiveness, grace, challenge, and triumph will inspire and sustain the reader through every bend in the road of life. Each short chapter is an instructional jewel clarifying the nuances of such topics as: Dealing with Low Energy, Seeing Spirit Everywhere, Finding Calmness in the Midst of Activity, and How to Enjoy Long Meditations. In this book you will discover how to balance the inner life of meditation with the outer life of work.

Faith Is My Armor
The Life of Swami Kriyananda
Devi Novak

The life of Swami Kriyananda is the story of a modern-day hero—a man who has achieved extraordinary victories by demonstrating spiritual courage, determination amid great obstacles, and personal sacrifice.

Faith Is My Armor tells the complete story of his life: from his childhood in Rumania, to his desperate search for meaning in life, and to his training under his great guru, the Indian master, Paramhansa Yogananda.

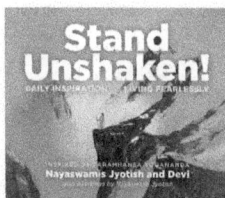

Stand Unshaken!

Daily Inspiration for Living Fearlessly
Nayaswami Jyotish and Nayaswami Devi

"You must stand unshaken amidst the crash of breaking worlds!" It was Paramhansa Yogananda who issued this soul-stirring exhortation. How do we follow his great example and become warriors for the Light? *Stand Unshaken!* offers inspiration and practical guidance on how to live courageously during these turbulent times. Each secret of living fearlessly (one for each day of the month) is paired with a beautiful painting by Nayaswami Jyotish. Awaken within you the power to live in joy whatever your outward circumstances, stand unshaken, and become a true light unto the world.

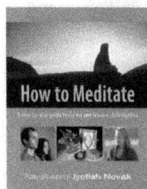

How to Meditate

A Step-by-Step Guide to the Art & Science of Meditation
Jyotish Novak

This clear and concise guidebook contains everything you need to start your practice. With easy-to-follow instructions, meditation teacher Jyotish Novak demystifies meditation—presenting the essential techniques so that you can quickly grasp them. How to Meditate has helped thousands to establish a regular meditation routine since it was first published in 1989. This newly revised edition includes a bonus chapter on scientific studies showing the benefits of meditation, plus all-new photographs and illustrations.

"The clearest, most practical, and most inspiring guide on meditation I've ever read." —**Joseph Bharat Cornell,** meditation instructor, author of *Sharing Nature*

"Meditation is a complicated term for something that is truly simple. **How To Meditate** is a guide to mastering meditation and reaping more of the benefit of the serenity of the matter. With tips on finding relaxation, opening your natural intuition, and more, this book is a must for those who want to unlock their spirituality." —**Midwest Book Review**

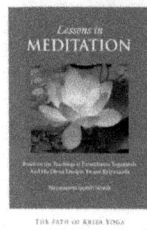

Lessons in Meditation

Jyotish Novak

Small but powerful, this book concisely presents Paramhansa Yogananda's basic spiritual practices, including exercises for relaxation, energization, concentration, meditation, visualization, chanting, and prayer, with simple, "doable" suggestions. These lessons offer the preliminary techniques of Kriya Yoga, including the *Hong-Sau* concentration technique and Yoganandaji's Energization Exercises for strengthening the body and will power.

Divine Wisdom

The Original Writings of
Paramhansa Yogananda

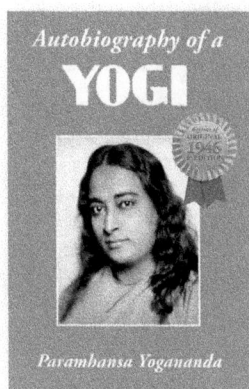

THE ORIGINAL 1946 UNEDITED EDITION OF
YOGANANDA'S SPIRITUAL MASTERPIECE

Autobiography of a Yogi
Paramhansa Yogananda

Autobiography of a Yogi is one of the world's most acclaimed spiritual classics, with millions of copies sold. Named one of the Best 100 Spiritual Books of the twentieth century, this book helped launch and continues to inspire a spiritual awakening throughout the Western world.

Yogananda was the first yoga master of India whose mission brought him to settle and teach in the West. His firsthand account of his life experiences in India includes childhood revelations, stories of his visits to saints and masters, and long-secret teachings of yoga and Self-realization that he first made available to the Western reader.

This reprint of the original 1946 edition is free from textual changes made after Yogananda's passing in 1952. This updated edition includes bonus materials: the last chapter that Yogananda wrote in 1951, also without posthumous changes, the eulogy Yogananda wrote for Gandhi, and a new foreword and afterword by Swami Kriyananda, one of Yogananda's close, direct disciples.

Scientific Healing Affirmations
Paramhansa Yogananda

Yogananda's 1924 classic, reprinted here, is a pioneering work in the fields of self-healing and self-transformation. He explains that words are crystallized thoughts and have life-changing power when spoken with conviction, concentration, willpower, and feeling. Yogananda offers far more than mere suggestions for achieving positive attitudes. He shows how to impregnate words with spiritual force to shift habitual thought patterns of the mind and create a new personal reality.

Added to this text are over fifty of Yogananda's well-loved "Short Affirmations," taken from issues of *East-West* and *Inner Culture* magazines from 1932 to 1942. This little book will be a treasured companion on the road to realizing your highest, divine potential.

Metaphysical Meditations
Paramhansa Yogananda

Metaphysical Meditations is a classic collection of meditation techniques, visualizations, affirmations, and prayers from the great yoga master, Paramhansa Yogananda. The meditations given are of three types: those spoken to the individual consciousness, prayers or demands addressed to God, and affirmations that bring us closer to the Divine.

Select a passage that meets your specific need and speak each word slowly and purposefully until you become absorbed in its inner meaning. At the bedside, by the meditation seat, or while traveling—one can choose no better companion than *Metaphysical Meditations*.

~THE WISDOM of YOGANANDA~

This series features writings of Paramhansa Yogananda not available elsewhere—including many from his earliest years in America—in an approachable, easy-to-read format. The words of the Master are presented with minimal editing, to capture his expansive and compassionate wisdom, his sense of fun, and his practical guidance.

How to Be Happy All the Time
The Wisdom of Yogananda Series, VOLUME 1

Yogananda explains everything needed to lead a happier, more fulfilling life. Topics include: looking for happiness in the right places; choosing to be happy; tools, techniques, and methods for achieving happiness; sharing happiness with others; and balancing success with happiness.

Karma and Reincarnation
The Wisdom of Yogananda Series, VOLUME 2

Yogananda reveals the reality of karma, death, reincarnation, and the afterlife. With clarity and simplicity, he makes the mysterious understandable: why we see a world of suffering and inequality; what happens at death and after death; the purpose of reincarnation; and how to handle the challenges we face in our lives.

How to Love and Be Loved
The Wisdom of Yogananda Series, VOLUME 3

Yogananda shares practical guidance and fresh insight on relationships of all types: how to cure friendship-ending habits; how to choose the right partner; the role of sex in marriage; how to conceive a spiritually oriented child; the solutions to problems that arise in marriage; and the Universal Love at the heart of all relationships.

How to Be a Success
The Wisdom of Yogananda Series, VOLUME 4

This book includes the complete text of *The Attributes of Success,* the original booklet later published as *The Law of Success.* In addition, you will learn how to find your purpose in life, develop habits of success, eradicate habits of failure, develop will power and magnetism, and thrive in the right job.

How to Have Courage, Calmness, and Confidence
The Wisdom of Yogananda Series, VOLUME 5
Winner of the 2011 International Book Award for Best Self-Help Title

A master at helping people change and grow, Yogananda shows how to transform one's life: dislodge negative thoughts and depression; uproot fear and thoughts of failure; cure nervousness and systematically eliminate worry from life; and overcome anger, sorrow, oversensitivity, and a host of other troublesome emotions.

How to Achieve Glowing Health and Vitality
The Wisdom of Yogananda Series, VOLUME 6

Yogananda explains principles that promote physical health and overall well-being, mental clarity, and inspiration in one's spiritual life. He offers practical, wide-ranging, and fascinating suggestions on having more energy and living a radiantly healthy life. Readers will discover the priceless Energization Exercises for rejuvenating the body and mind, the fine art of conscious relaxation, and helpful diet tips for health and beauty.

How to Awaken Your True Potential
The Wisdom of Yogananda Series, VOLUME 7

With compassion, humor, and deep understanding of human psychology, Yogananda offers instruction on releasing limitations to access the power of mind and heart. Discover your hidden resources and be empowered to choose a life with greater meaning, purpose, and joy.

The Man Who Refused Heaven
The Wisdom of Yogananda Series, VOLUME 8

Why is humor so deeply appreciated? Laughter is one of the great joys of life. Joy is fundamental to who we are. The humor in this book is taken from Yogananda's writings. Also included are experiences with the Master that demonstrate his playful spirit.

How to Face Life's Changes
The Wisdom of Yogananda Series, VOLUME 9

Changes come not to destroy us, rather, to help us grow in understanding and to learn the lessons we must to reach our highest potential. Guided by Yogananda, tap into the changeless joy of your soul-nature, empowering you to move through life fearlessly and with an open heart. Learn to accept change as the reality of life; face change in relationships, finances, and health with gratitude; and cultivate key attitudes like fearlessness, non-attachment, and willpower.

How to Spiritualize Your Life
The Wisdom of Yogananda Series, VOLUME 10

Yogananda answers a diverse range of questions asked by truth-seekers, sharing his teachings and insights on how to be successful in the everyday world and in one's spiritual life. Addressing financial, physical, mental, emotional, and spiritual challenges, he explains how best to expand one's consciousness and live life to the fullest. Compiled from his articles, lessons, and handwritten letters, this tenth volume in the Wisdom of Yogananda series was written in a question-and-answer format, well suited to both individual and group study.

How to Live Without Fear

The Wisdom of Yogananda Series, VOLUME 11

Releases: January 2024

~ ~ ~ ~ ~ ~ ~ ~

Whispers from Eternity

Paramhansa Yogananda
Edited by his disciple, Swami Kriyananda

Many poetic works can inspire, but few, like this one, have the power to change your life. Yogananda was not only a spiritual master, but a master poet, whose verses revealed the hidden divine presence behind even everyday things. He felt that this book belonged among his chief literary contributions. As he wrote once in a poem, "When I am only a dream, Read my *Whispers from Eternity*; Eternally through it I will talk to you."

Moments of Truth, Volume One

Excerpts from the Rubaiyat of Omar Khayyam Explained
Paramhansa Yogananda

"One day, as I was deeply concentrated on the pages of Omar Khayyam's *Rubaiyat*, I suddenly beheld the walls of its outer meanings crumble away. Lo! vast inner meanings opened like a golden treasure house before my gaze." —Paramhansa Yogananda

Moments of Truth, Volume One is the first in a series of small books of excerpts from the teachings of Paramhansa Yogananda, as set forth in his own books and in those of his close disciple, Swami Kriyananda.

The gems of wisdom in this little volume are taken from Yogananda's commentaries on *The Rubaiyat of Omar Khayyam*, considered by Westerners a celebration of earthly pleasures, but widely recognized in the East as a work of profound spirituality. Yogananda's commentaries are a true scripture in their own right. These selections have scripture's power to change your consciousness, and your life.

From the book: "Behold this one flaming truth: All life is fleeting. Cling to that understanding, and seek, then, within yourself that which alone endures."

Paramhansa Yogananda: A Biography

With personal reflections and reminiscences by Swami Kriyananda

Paramhansa Yogananda's classic *Autobiography of a Yogi* is more about the saints Yogananda met than about himself—in spite of the fact that Yogananda was much greater than many he described. One of Yogananda's closest direct disciples relates here the untold story of this great spiritual master and world teacher: his teenage miracles, his challenges in coming to America, his national lecture campaigns, his struggles to fulfill his world-changing mission amid incomprehension and painful betrayals, and his ultimate triumphant achievement. Kriyananda's subtle grasp of his guru's inner nature reveals Yogananda's many-sided greatness. Includes many never-before-published anecdotes.

"Swami Kriyananda's biography is a welcome addition to the growing literature on Paramhansa Yogananda. I especially like the author's chapter on Yogananda's legacy where he quotes Yogananda on his concept of 'world brotherhood colonies.' I am astounded to find that a consciousness-based theory of evolution predicts the evolutionary necessity of such colonies. Yogananda was a true seer and indeed, his words 'shall not die.'" —**Amit Goswami, PhD**, quantum physicist and author of *The Self-Aware Universe, Creative Evolution, and How Quantum Activism Can Save Civilization*

The New Path

My Life with Paramhansa Yogananda
Swami Kriyananda

Winner of the 2010 Eric Hoffer Award for Best Self-Help/Spiritual Book
Winner of the 2010 USA Book News Award for Best Spiritual Book

This is the moving story of Kriyananda's years with Paramhansa Yogananda, India's emissary to the West and the first yoga master to spend the greater part of his life in America. When Swami Kriyananda discovered *Autobiography of a Yogi* in 1948, he was totally new to Eastern teachings. This is a great advantage to the Western reader, since Kriyananda walks us along the yogic path as he discovers it from the moment of his initiation as a disciple of Yogananda. With winning honesty, humor, and deep insight, he shares his journey on the spiritual path through personal stories and experiences.

Through more than four hundred stories of life with Yogananda, we tune in more deeply to this great master and to the teachings he brought to the West. This book is an ideal complement to *Autobiography of a Yogi*.

Conversations with Yogananda

Stories, Sayings, and Wisdom of Paramhansa Yogananda
Recorded, with reflections by his disciple,
Swami Kriyananda

For those who enjoyed Paramhansa Yogananda's autobiography and long for more, this collection of conversations offers rare intimate glimpses of life with the Master as never before shared.

This is an unparalleled account of Yogananda and his teachings written by one of his foremost disciples. Swami Kriyananda was often present when Yogananda spoke privately with other close disciples, received visitors and answered their questions, and dictated and discussed his writings. He recorded the Master's words, preserving a treasure trove of wisdom that would otherwise have been lost.

These Conversations include not only Yogananda's words as he spoke them, but the added insight of a disciple who spent over fifty years attuning his consciousness to that of his guru.

The collection features nearly five hundred stories, sayings, and insights from the twenthieth century's most famous master of yoga, as well as twenty-five photos—nearly all previously unreleased.

The Essence of Self-Realization

The Wisdom of Paramhansa Yogananda
Recorded, compiled, and edited by his disciple,
Swami Kriyananda

Filled with lessons, stories, and jewels of wisdom that Paramhansa Yogananda shared only with his closest disciples, this volume is an invaluable guide to the spiritual life, carefully organized in twenty main topics.

Great teachers work through their students, and Yogananda was no exception. Swami Kriyananda comments, "After I'd been with him a year and a half, he began urging me to write down the things he was saying during informal conversations." Many of the three hundred sayings presented here are available nowhere else. This book and *Conversations with Yogananda* are must-reads for anyone wishing to know more about Yogananda's teachings and to absorb his wisdom.

*"Be assured that at each sitting, whether for one page or one chapter, you will have gleaned some refreshment for a tired heart or a thirsty soul. . . . Essence is easy to read, besides being quite a bit of fun." — **Spirit of Change Magazine***

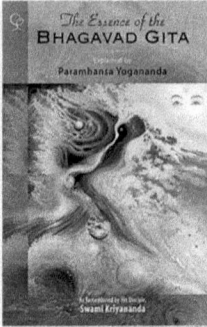

The Essence of the Bhagavad Gita

Explained by Paramhansa Yogananda
As remembered by his disciple, Swami Kriyananda

Rarely in a lifetime does a new spiritual classic appear that has the power to change people's lives and transform future generations. This is such a book.

This revelation of India's best-loved scripture approaches it from a fresh perspective, showing its deep allegorical meaning and its down-to-earth practicality. The themes presented are universal: how to achieve victory in life in union with the divine; how to prepare for life's "final exam," death, and what happens afterward; how to triumph over all pain and suffering.

"It is doubtful that there has been a more important spiritual writing in the last fifty years than this soul-stirring, monumental work. What a gift! What a treasure!" —**Neale Donald Walsch**, author of *Conversations with God*

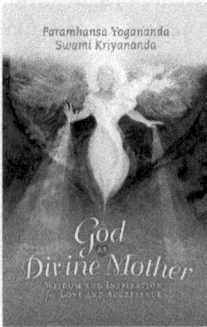

God as Divine Mother

Wisdom and Inspiration for Love and Acceptance
Paramhansa Yogananda and Swami Kriyananda

We long for a God who loves us exactly as we are, who doesn't judge us but rather helps and encourages us in achieving our highest potential. In this book, discover the teachings and inspirations on Divine Mother from Paramhansa Yogananda. These teachings are universal: No matter your religious background, or lack thereof, you will find these messages of love and acceptance resonating on a soul-level. Included also are over thirty poems and prayers dedicated to God in the form of Divine Mother, and original chants and songs by the authors.